Teaching Children Foreign Languages

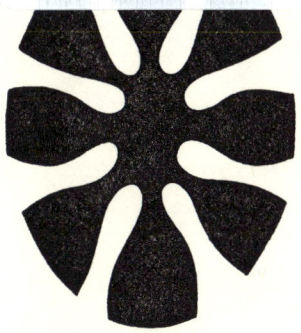

MARY FINOCCHIARO, Ph.D.

Director, Foreign Language Institute for Elementary School Teachers
Hunter College of the City University of New York

Specialist, Language and Linguistics, U.S. Department of State

Formerly, Principal, Elementary Schools
Formerly, Chairman Language Department
Secondary Schools, New York City

Andrew S. Thomas Memorial Library
MORRIS HARVEY COLLEGE, CHARLESTON, W. VA.

McGRAW–HILL BOOK COMPANY, New York · San Francisco · Toronto · London

567891011 BP 10.

TEACHING CHILDREN FOREIGN LANGUAGES

Copyright © 1964 by McGraw-Hill, Inc.
All Rights Reserved. Printed in the United States of America.
This book, or parts thereof, may not be reproduced in any form without permission of the publishers.

Library of Congress Catalog Card Number 64–19210

Foreword

There is no question in the minds of national leaders in the United States and abroad that the knowledge of a second or even a third language is of prime importance. The mastery of another language is no longer thought of as a cultural adornment; it is considered a major psychological weapon. A look at educational budgets of many countries throughout the world indicates that each year provisions are included for increased expenditures for language learning. Our Federal government realizes this and has provided almost a billion dollars for the stimulation of science, mathematics, and foreign languages.

The urgency of a knowledge of foreign languages is apparent to all. How can the need be met—quickly and effectively?

The inadequacy of foreign language teaching in our country heretofore has been due largely to two major weaknesses: too late and too little. Most students did not learn the language until they reached high school, and the great majority pursued the subject for only two years. Everyone, however, knows that learning a language is a long process, extending over many years and requiring constant practice.

The simplest, the most natural, and the most effective way of learning a language is to begin early. The young child's speech organs are flexible; his mind is uninhibited. He takes a natural delight in learning new speech patterns, and he imitates readily. Pedagogically and psychologically, the reasons for teaching young children a foreign language and the culture of the people who speak that language are of the soundest.

The present volume will provide teachers and administrators with the theory and practice necessary for introducing effective programs in the elementary schools and for stimulating in children the desire to pursue the study of languages.

Theodore Huebener

Preface

Assignments in Europe, Africa, and Asia from which I have just returned have underscored sharply the truth of former United States Education Commissioner Earl McGrath's statement that "the greatest educational challenge of our time is to determine how our schools and colleges can train mature, resourceful, world-minded young Americans capable of assuming unprecedented international responsibilities."

I had occasion to talk to numerous native English speakers who are abroad on educational, business, or governmental missions. Many of them did not know the language of the country in which they were working and had reason to bemoan that fact bitterly. They were certain that their effectiveness would have been increased a hundredfold by an understanding and speaking knowledge of the language, however small. They felt they were at the mercy of well-meaning interpreters who—either because they did not understand the subject under discussion or because they placed a totally different meaning on a word or concept—did not convey the exact message to their listeners.

I will not mention the fortunately small group who felt indignant that the people in the host country had not learned their language to prepare for their coming. Even more resentful were those who kept repeating "I had two years of language in high school, but I can't say a word."

As important as these reactions may be, the comments of the nationals of the countries to which American and British personnel are assigned have even greater significance. In general, they are grateful for assistance in any form. Many of these beneficiaries, however, would be even more grateful to hear a few halting words in their own language. The attempt on our part to communicate with them in their language would convince them more than money or equipment that we are interested in them as people with a language and culture as important as our own.

It is obvious, too, that this attempt at an understanding of the other person's values and goals is necessary on several levels, not on the diplomatic level alone.

The members of the diplomatic corps are highly respected, with very few exceptions. More and more of them are making a sincere effort to gain a knowledge of the language. They initiate many cultural activities which underscore the reciprocal cultural values of both countries.

The impression created by thousands of other assigned persons and their families, however, is unfortunately more lasting. How very often I heard "He's been here a year and has never tried to learn a word." It is this apparent lack of effort toward learning their language which disturbs the nationals.

On the other side of the coin, I am pleased to say that one of my assignments in Europe was to speak at a conference sponsored by the United States Air Force. Here steps were being taken to teach Air Force personnel the language of the country to which they had been assigned. The proposal was received with enthusiasm by Air Force education advisers. Materials are now in preparation so that the proposal may become a reality.

The Air Force project is one of numerous efforts being made by the United States government, for example, to make sure that some of its personnel stationed abroad will have the ability to communicate with the people with whom they live and work. Of necessity, the programs will require a large outlay of money. They will also demand a great expenditure of time and effort on the part of the learners. Although these learners will be highly motivated and will have the advantage of living in the country where the language is spoken, the majority of them are past the age when learning a language is child's play.

It is evident that more needs to be done to eradicate the image of disinterest that too many native English speakers abroad present. The importance of communication and understanding on a people-to-people level can no longer be questioned.

Immediate measures should be taken to develop functional second language skills in a large segment of the English-speaking population. Experimentation and observation indicate that these skills can be developed most easily and successfully and with the least expense at the elementary school level.

Much is being done to accomplish this end at the present time. In the United States, for example, there are at present nearly 2 million language learners at the elementary school level. Educational and lay leaders continue to meet to discuss the possibility of initiating foreign language programs in the elementary schools. Many are starting experimental programs in selected schools.

Giant steps have already been taken in this field by a few farsighted men and women who defied inertia and tradition to develop the world-minded Americans the nation so desperately needs. These educational leaders were cognizant of the fact that an acceptance of the language and customs of others could best be inculcated in youngsters during the formative period of their lives.

This book is respectfully dedicated to them.

It is a privilege to be able to acknowledge the inspiration and helpful suggestions that I have always received from Dr. Theodore Huebener, director of foreign languages, Board of Education, New York City. I am grateful, too, to Mrs. Renée McGee of Georgetown University and to Miss Remunda Cadoux, consultant in foreign languages to the New York State Education Department, for their reading of portions of the manuscript and for their guidance.

Mary Finocchiaro

CONTENTS

Foreword v
Preface vii

CHAPTER 1 *What Are Some Facts about Language Teaching in the Elementary Schools?* **1**

Introduction 1
Self-evident Truths 3
Problems—All Solvable 5

CHAPTER 2 *What Knowledge and Attitudes Should the Teacher Possess?* **21**

Introduction 21
The Nature of Language 22
Goals of Language Learning
 in the Elementary Schools 24
Principles of Language Learning 26
The Teacher's Role 30
Sources of Help 32
Some Intangibles 33

CHAPTER 3 *What Should Be Taught?* **35**

Introduction 35
Selecting the Material 36
 Cultural Topics 38
 Language Items for Intensive Practice 41
 Organizing the Course Content 49
 Integrating Topic and Language
  Items by Grade or Level 56

CHAPTER 4 **How Are Language Skills Developed?**   **58**

    Multiple Approaches   58
    The Sequence of Development   66
    Developing Aural-Oral Abilities   67
    Developing Reading Skills   80
    Developing Writing Skills   82
    General Procedures and Suggestions:
        Some Comments   83
        Teaching Pronunciation   83
        Presenting Language Items   85
        Activities Resulting in Language Learning   88

CHAPTER 5 **How Can Teaching Be Made Effective?**   **95**

    Creating a Favorable Learning Environment   95
    Planning for Learning   99
    Vitalizing Learning   105
    Correlating Language and Other
        Curriculum Areas   132
    Evaluating the Program—Articulation
        with Secondary Schools   135

CHAPTER 6 **How Should Materials Be Prepared?**   **141**

    Introduction   141
    Basic Assumptions   142
    Decisions and Responsibilities   148
    Minimum Essentials   152
    A Checklist for Curriculum Writers   155

    SAMPLE MATERIALS   *158*
    Dialogues   159
    Other Materials   161

    SOURCES AND RESOURCES FOR TEACHERS   *192*
    FL PROGRAM NOTES STANDARDS FOR
        TEACHER–EDUCATION PROGRAMS IN
        MODERN FOREIGN LANGUAGES   *198*
    GLOSSARY OF USEFUL TERMS   *201*
    INDEX   *207*

TEACHING CHILDREN FOREIGN LANGUAGES

1

What Are Some Facts about Language Teaching in the Elementary Schools?

INTRODUCTION

The need for people with proficiency in more than one language is recognized by all those concerned with their country's representation and commitments abroad and aware of the need for communication with the many non-native speakers of English residing within their own country. Generally recognized, too, is the fact that a long sequence of learning is needed to produce language proficiency. There is increasing awareness of the physical and psychological advantages of an early start in language study.

Despite these facts and although many school systems have introduced foreign languages in the elementary school, some administrators and citizens still question the advisability of offering a second language to children. In some instances, their doubts are based on the report of a vocal parent on the school board who told them that her friend's child said, "All we do in the language class is color a map of France." In others, their doubts persist because parents had visited a community where language was being taught and had observed a poor teacher. Granted that these facts may be true—and we do not doubt them for a minute—the answer is not to do away with languages, but to prepare teachers for new responsibilities, to set realistic and attainable goals in the elementary schools, to inform parents what these goals are, to prepare adequate instructional materials, to ensure a smooth and continuous program with the secondary schools, and to evaluate and improve the program continuously.

Administrators who are responsible to the community express other concerns as well. These are related to pupil selection, scheduling, costs, or personnel. We will examine some of these and other areas of concern briefly in this chapter in order to separate the facts from the myths about language teaching in the elementary school.

Myths invariably develop around new trends in education sometimes because overenthusiastic educators claim too much for a new theory or approach and sometimes because teachers in service are not always given the orientation and knowledge which would help them make a new program more effective.

Experience has shown that teachers do not resist change if carefully planned orientation enables them to incorporate new ideas into their teaching while retaining the feeling of security that is so necessary in the classroom. Some of us will recall with chagrin and frustration the directives to teachers which characterized "acceptance" of the generally misunderstood activity program. "Teach the whole child" and "Go in and meet the needs of your pupils" were clichés not usually followed by specific directions or by examples of desirable practices. Good teachers responded by reading, by asking questions, perhaps by adding some new approaches to their traditional teaching. Less competent or disinterested teachers found themselves confused and becoming even poorer teachers. "Meet the needs" was interpreted to mean "Don't prepare lesson plans"; "Teach the whole child" was often interpreted to mean "Let the children do whatever they wish in order not to produce emotional or social blocks."

Fortunately the kind of confusion suggested above need not arise in the Foreign Language Elementary School (FLES) program. There is a growing body of excellent materials which can point the way for teachers, administrators, and an interested public. FLES should no longer be considered in the experimental stage. Reports of successful programs are available in numerous periodicals and journals. Instead of starting completely anew, school systems and individual teachers should accept what has already been tried in the field. They should build on an already established base, experimenting further, adapting materials, or varying or adding some elements which may be especially pertinent to their learning situation.

Never in our history has there been a more pressing need for more language learning by more children in more schools; nor does the urgency of the moment permit long delay or elaborate preparations. In order to meet this unprecedented need, many communities will have to bypass the pilot-project stage and plunge into effective large-scale programs. But these programs will be effective only if pupils, parents, and administrators accept them. The key person who can bring this acceptance about is the teacher. It is what he does with his pupils and with the available resources—people as well as instructional materials—that will determine pupil and community acceptance and program effectiveness.

This book, then, is directed primarily to the teacher and to the administrator who wants to provide as much help to the teacher as possible. In harmony with the philosophy expressed above of building on what has been tried successfully, examples of classroom practices and materials that have been subjected to the test of actual use for many years will be given in this book, together with samples or models of materials exactly as they were used.

A brief chapter will be devoted to the principles and procedures underlying the preparation or adaptation of classroom materials. None of these will find their way into classrooms unless you are convinced that foreign language study has as much place in the curriculum as social studies, for example. Let us first, therefore, look at some of the facts about teaching languages in the elementary schools.

SELF-EVIDENT TRUTHS

1. Increasing international involvement, expanding business interests in newly established nations, constantly improving travel facilities and the resulting growth of tourism, the growing interchange among nations of scientific and technological information—all will add to the number of people traveling or working outside their homelands. Impressive statistics concerning the large numbers involved in these activities have been compiled by others and will not be repeated here.

2. These same factors have created and will continue to create an increased demand for bilingual or trilingual personnel.

3. Skilled language teachers are required for the development of adequate language competency in the people who will be needed to fill the growing number of posts. The existing shortage of language teachers threatens to become even more acute.

4. Today there is consensus that both an understanding and a speaking knowledge of a foreign language are essential for communication, whereas in the past, a reading or writing knowledge was considered the main objective of language study or perhaps all one could hope to achieve in the usual language program. Scientists, for example, who used to feel that a reading knowledge of a language was sufficient, find that attendance at the numerous international conferences which are part of today's way of life makes understanding as well as speaking a most desirable asset.

5. The ability to understand and speak, as well as to read and write, cannot be acquired in the two- or three-year sequence in secondary schools which has been offered in the majority of communities up to now.

6. A longer sequence of study is essential in order to develop reasonable facility in the language skills. Since many of our secondary school students may not enter college, the longer time sequence will have to be achieved by starting the study of a foreign language in the elementary schools.

7. Childhood is the ideal period for acquiring a native or near-native pronunciation. Medical evidence, experimentation, and objective observation have proven conclusively that children learn foreign languages more quickly and more accurately (at least as far as pronunciation is concerned) than adolescents or adults because of the flexibility of their speech organs, their lack of the inhibitions that are typical of older persons learning a language, and their apparent physiological and psychological need to communicate with other children.

8. To children, a new way of expressing themselves, particularly if it is associated with a normal class activity, presents no problem. Children make no attempt to analyze language as adolescents or adults do. They do not immediately compare what they hear or say in the new language to English. They experience no conflict because of similar or completely dissimilar language items in English. They do not look for difficulties. They even use the dreaded subjunctives as normally and naturally as they would use the present tense of the verb "to have."

9. Childhood is the best time to acquire the beginnings of goodwill and intercultural understanding. Children are singularly free of prejudice, and enjoyable classroom or out-of-class experiences which familiarize them with the customs or mores of another country create

lasting impressions. Concomitant outcomes of their language study are the appreciation of the basic oneness of all mankind and the realization that differences between peoples do not signify either superiority or inferiority.

10. The current emphases on understanding and speaking the language and on developing cultural pluralism require new approaches, materials, and teaching skills. The teacher's major role in the new program (known as audio-lingual, audio-oral, or aural-oral) differs from the one he played when reading and writing skills were stressed. His major role today, particularly at the elementary level, is to engage pupils in pleasurable, varied practice so that their understanding and speaking—and later their reading and writing—of the authentic foreign language will be natural and habitual.

Since the teacher's function in the learning process constitutes the central theme of this text, we will set aside any discussion of it for the moment and briefly consider instead the problems—some real, some magnified—of introducing foreign languages in the elementary schools.

PROBLEMS—ALL SOLVABLE

In weighing the advisability of introducing any program into the school, the administrator must consider the pupils, the staff, the existing school program and facilities, and the community. Factors within each of these components require separate study, although they are interdependent in the actual school situation. What are some of the questions he must ask—questions whose answers have covered innumerable pages of the literature, questions that are still the subject of endless discussions among foreign language teachers and administrators or lay leaders? They are usually expressed as follows:
Which pupils should be selected for language study?
Where will we find teachers?
What will we "take out" of the curriculum in order to teach language?
In which grade should we introduce language study?
What problems of articulation will exist?
How can we give credit for language study?
What language should we teach?
How can we justify the cost of the program to the community?

These are all valid questions. They do require discussion and a point of view based on facts. Some of our arguments under each question may appear too pat and simple. We do not guarantee that the suggested solutions will work in your community, but we do urge you to use them as starting points for discussion, for further reading, and for gentle persuasion of interested (or disinterested) groups.

The Selection of Pupils In the program envisaged here, *all* children in regular classes would learn a foreign language.

If we do not merely pay lip service to the concept of equal educational opportunities for all children, it behooves us not to be selective. All children who have the mental ability to learn any subject in the curriculum will be able to profit from studying a foreign language. (Indeed, some interesting experimentation in this area reveals that even feebleminded persons are capable of understanding and speaking a second language.[1])

In addition, numerous reports indicate that many children who have not done particularly well in school have made rapid progress in language. More important, their feelings of success in that area contributed to general improvement in all areas.

It is specious reasoning to assume that some children will never need to use another language. Such reasoning is a throwback to the era when only the most affluent traveled abroad. Not only can we not predict what the status of pupils will be ten or fifteen years from now, but also, as pointed out above, when pupils are grown, they may be asked to serve in governmental or other posts in which knowledge of a foreign language may be required and certainly will be desirable.

Today's pattern of mobility and migration often results in everyday contacts between groups having different native languages—contacts which would be immeasurably improved by the inclusion of the appropriate second language in the curriculum. Three advantages immediately come to mind. First, the integration of newcomers into a community would be accelerated if the children understood each other and could play together. Second, the problems that always beset the second generation of immigrant families would be mitigated if the children took pride in their parents' language and customs, which certainly would be the case if their language were offered in the school. Third, the children whose native language is not English could take an active part in helping their classmates learn the second language. Consider the feeling of status that the children would gain by being

---

[1] Paul Angiolillo, "French for the Feebleminded: an experiment," *Modern Language Journal*, April, 1942, pp. 266–271.

able to help their classmates—a feeling desperately needed by children who may have been uprooted from their environment. These same advantages would accrue in situations such as the southwestern part of the United States or in Canada, where persons of different cultural backgrounds have lived together for many decades but where the children may come to school with little or no knowledge of the English language or culture.

This viewpoint and plan must be modified in certain circumstances, however. In the southwestern United States, for example, many Spanish-speaking children have no acquaintance with English when they enter school. If these children attend a school in which French is the only second language being offered, it is logical and desirable to exclude them *temporarily* from the foreign language program. They have an urgent need to learn English as quickly as possible in order to participate effectively in the total school program. (It is hoped, however, that in communities where there are many Spanish-speaking people, Spanish will be offered as one of the second languages in the elementary school.[2]

Children who have some knowledge of English—although they may not know English very well—should *not* be excluded from the language program. As noted above, there are reciprocal benefits to be derived from their presence in a class in which their native language is being taught.

If the foreign language is not their native tongue, they should still be permitted to join it with their classmates as soon as their knowledge of English is considered adequate for their participation in the other curriculum areas. Complete mastery should not be required of these children before they are allowed to join the second or third language class. Experience has demonstrated that most children are able to learn more than one new language without "interference" or harm to themselves. If one of the language classes is Spanish, their study of cognates and similar or contrasting structures will be helpful in their learning of English. More important, their success in Spanish may provide a strong motivating force to do well in other areas of learning.

The Teacher Shortage Many administrative arrangements are possible to meet the urgent need for teachers.

[2] This concept would be equally valid in Canada, for example, where French is the native "home" language of many children, or in Australia where Italian is the native tongue of many recent immigrants.

In some schools, the teacher who knows the foreign language teaches the language not only to his class but also to other classes in the school. His colleagues take his class for subjects such as art, music, health education, or other areas in which they may be specialists. A team-teaching principle is utilized. An obvious disadvantage of this arrangement is that the classroom teacher who is "relieved" of his class does not learn along with his pupils and, more important—unless there are frequent planning conferences between language teacher and classroom teacher—may be unaware of the experiences his pupils have had in the language class. He can thus provide little or no follow-up. Moreover, the possibilities of correlation of language with the other curricular areas, an important aspect of FLES, are neglected or minimized.

In some schools, a roving specialist sent either by the board of education or by a nearby college visits the school one or more times a week and teaches the new language items to the children in the school. Where possible, the same specialist visits the same school more than once a week in order to engage the children in follow-up activities. In other instances, the classroom teacher who has remained in the classroom while the specialist teaches the lesson engages in the follow-up practice activities with his class. Through this arrangement, the classroom teacher is also able to learn or to increase his knowledge of the language along with his pupils.

Nearby colleges help to relieve the foreign language teacher shortage by assigning student teachers to the elementary schools. The student teachers may be prospective secondary school teachers who have majored in the foreign language or prospective elementary school teachers who either have a foreign language background or have studied the language as a major or minor field. The supervision of the student teachers remains a cooperative undertaking of school administrator, college supervisor, and classroom teacher.

In the United States, teacher certification requirements may serve as examples for the preparation of the teachers of the future in this area. New York State certification requires elementary school teachers to offer a concentration in one subject area in their undergraduate studies. Thus they will be specialists in some curriculum area, as well as generalists. As more persons become aware of the urgency for teaching foreign languages, many young people will be channeled into foreign language study as their area of special concentration. Another certification requirement—while in the field of art—holds promise for other areas as well. Prospective secondary school teachers must do their student teaching in both the elementary and the secondary schools—thirty and ninety hours per semester, respectively. Their college supervisor works with school administrators and cooperating teachers in both schools in the supervision of the student teacher. This practice could be extended to the language field.

Even if schools cannot benefit immediately from the student-teaching program because there is no college in the vicinity, the two policies mentioned above should have far-reaching results. Elementary school teachers who have studied a language in depth as their area of concentration will be able to teach it effectively alone or as part of a team. Their knowledge of elementary school philosophy and a foreign language—to which we hope will be added in-service training in the *teaching* of a foreign language—will make them effective FLES teachers. A student teacher's experience in both elementary and secondary schools (as in the New York State art program) will invalidate the arguments (often given by elementary school personnel) that secondary school teachers are not aware of the objectives of the elementary school or of children's characteristics and needs. Any practice that promotes better understanding and smoother articulation is to be desired fervently.

Another administrative pattern for overcoming the shortage of trained teachers has been used successfully in several countries: A language teaching specialist meets weekly with all the teachers of a grade in any given district. During the session, usually lasting about two hours, the specialist helps the teachers acquire the accurate pronunciation, understanding, and use of the new language patterns to be taught *that week only.* The specialist may also suggest some of the follow-up activities, or grade committees in each school may prepare such activities under the specialist's or the administrator's direction. Sometimes, tapes and records of the materials practiced during the two-hour session are given to the teachers for home use. It goes without saying that such in-service training would be insufficient for the classroom teacher with *no* knowledge whatsoever of the foreign language. It is excellent, however, for imparting greater fluency—and confidence—to the teacher who has some knowledge of the language but is afraid to teach it.

Television and films for teacher-training purposes are utilized in many places. Their use is made a pleasurable school-wide or district-wide weekly activity; in some cases, they may be the basis of a two-week intensive seminar. A systematically planned in-service program of films and records designed to produce or increase language competency in teachers is desirable from many points of view. Teachers gain a skill which enables them to enrich their lives through cultural activities otherwise closed to them. In turn, they grow in professional competence and effectiveness because they can enrich their teaching with other tools, skills, and information.

The teacher shortage may also be overcome by the use of bilingual persons in the community—with or without professional training. Those without training act as "informants." Although the word "informant" is generally used to indicate a native speaker, the informant can be someone who has learned the language well and is not a trained teacher. Many such people are willing to serve in the schools without compensation. With the cooperation of the classroom teacher, they can make invaluable contributions to the foreign language program. At regularly scheduled meetings, the teacher tells the native speaker or informant what language items he would like taught that week. The informant repeats these items in the classroom numerous times, with pauses for repetition, until teacher and class learn them. The classroom teacher then carries out the follow-up activities.

At all times, the school staff, familiar with city and state syllabuses, determine which materials are to be taught, their selection based on the correlation of the language program with the other curriculum areas and their knowledge of the school-wide program. It is important to remember, however, that although it is the school staff which must make the final decision, it is advantageous to plan the scope and sequence of the program in cooperation with someone who knows the foreign language well, e.g., a classroom teacher, a college or board of education specialist, or a bilingual informant. The knowledge of such people—of language patterns which contrast most sharply with English, of items which are related, and of songs and games, for example—should be incorporated into the program.

Some school systems without adequately prepared teachers, specialists, or informants make extensive use of television programs, kinescopes, or films in teaching foreign language. These have been found effective only where the classroom teacher remains with his class and conducts follow-up practice activities.

The most desirable situation, of course, is the one in which the regular classroom teacher teaches the foreign language. In a few years, this suggestion should present no problem, since many colleges and school systems will undoubtedly require that prospective elementary school teachers know at least one foreign language well. Also, more young people who plan to teach will prepare themselves in a foreign language as they become increasingly aware that such training is necessary for effective elementary school teaching and that it also offers many additional opportunities for professional growth.

Qualifications of Teachers Let us examine another facet of the teacher problem. In the light of the existing shortage, the unpreparedness of many nations to meet this shortage immediately, what preparation can we expect the FLES "stopgap teachers" to have?

To persons accustomed to hearing that the standards for foreign language teachers should be raised and that the teacher must have a thorough knowledge of the foreign language, it may come as a shock to hear us advocate that until these are feasible, we should accept the premise that the teacher need not have a thorough knowledge of all the nuances of the foreign language and literature, desirable as such a thorough knowledge would be.

In today's approach to teaching language at *the beginning level,* it is deemed advisable, for reasons which will be explained in more detail in the next chapter, that the teacher use and repeat a limited number of sentence patterns and give the children intensive practice in those patterns only. The teacher should learn to pronounce these limited patterns as perfectly as possible; he should learn when to use them and with which other combinations they are normally used. He should learn how to develop and how to judge accurate pronunciation in his pupils. He should learn, too, how to give varied, interesting practice in the limited patterns being taught. Improvisation by teacher or pupils at this level is not recommended.

The accurate and fluent pronunciation of patterns needed for the beginning level can be gained by teachers who have some language background and are willing to devote some time each day to practice. There are hundreds of records, films, and tapes already on the market. In addition, neighboring colleges or secondary schools with language laboratory facilities are usually eager to help in the preparation of language tapes. After the school committee, in cooperation with a bilingual person, selects the language items to be presented and/or reviewed in each grade, a bilingual person in the community, the specialist from the board of education, or a member of the staff in the secondary school or college can prepare appropriate tapes. These tapes can serve a dual purpose. They can be used not only in teacher training but also in language classrooms to give children additional listening and speaking practice. The tapes present another advantage. Pupils will learn to understand the materials taught by their teacher when spoken by other voices. Becoming accustomed to many voices saying the same material is an important objective of language learning.

These are only a few of the possibilities for overcoming the temporary dearth of qualified teachers. Other possibilities will occur to you as you examine and tap the resources in your own community.

The Crowded Curriculum In the opinion of many, language has as much place in the curriculum at the present time as any other subject. Language study can make the same contributions toward meeting the educational objectives of the elementary school as can any other area of study. Indeed, if properly presented, it can reinforce the knowledge gained in areas such as social studies, arithmetic, music, or art, while making particular contributions toward the development of attitudes of understanding and appreciation of other peoples. A positive attitude is needed not only toward people in foreign lands but also toward non-English-speaking residents of our own country. Such attitudes are best developed in the elementary school.

Experts generally agree that in the third, fourth, and fifth grades, a fifteen- to twenty-minute language session each day (or at the very least, three times a week) will be adequate. In grade 6, half an hour should be devoted to language. This means that each of the seven or eight other subjects taught in the school day need be cut by only two or three minutes. Certainly this could be done without serious damage to the other subject areas! If we believe that foreign language study has a place in the elementary schools, then economies can be effected during the school day in many ways. Routine matters can be relegated to routines; teaching can start as soon as wraps are removed in the morning; the morning milk break can be cut by a minute or two or even made part of the language period. Although teachers and students usually report at 8:40, instruction does not begin until about 9 A.M. That sometimes aimless twenty-minute period could be turned to good advantage.

When to Begin Many schools begin language study in the third grade. By the third grade, all children have become accustomed to school routines, have learned to read and write English, have gotten

Some Facts about Language Teaching in the Elementary Schools 13

past the readiness stage in the English-language arts and in mathematics. The third-grade curriculum in many countries begins to explore the wider community; children learn how people in other parts of the world live. The material of the Modern Language Association of America, for example, assumes a third-year starting point.

Some language specialists believe that language study should begin in kindergarten or the first grade. The author's experience, as principal of an elementary school, in teaching French in the first, third, and sixth grades demonstrated clearly that the first graders retained most, imitated most accurately, and most enjoyed talking in the new language about their classroom activities. They took particular pride in talking about the experiential material they were using in the mathematics-readiness program, for example.

In this, as in many other questions related to education, there is no *one* right answer. The major factors which warrant consideration are three:

How many "prepared" teachers or competent bilingual persons in the community are available?

Do the pupils require many readiness experiences to develop the basic concepts they need in the English-language-arts program, or have they come to school with a sufficiently broad experiential background?

Does the English-speaking community, for example, have within it a large group of non-English-speaking children?

In this last case, it may be desirable—even in the first grade—to offer an intensive program in English for the non-English-speaking group and to teach the language of that group to the English-speaking group. The reasons for recommending such an arrangement are obvious.

In general, however, a starting point in the third year appears educationally justifiable at this time. It is hoped that as school systems gain more experience in FLES, an earlier starting point will be considered. In that case, the FLES curriculum will have to be reevaluated carefully so that the six-year program will not become a diluted version of the four-year program now generally offered.

Language in the School Day The number of minutes and the time during the school day for the new language experience will also depend on several factors. In grades 1 to 5, the usual period is twenty minutes a day; in grade 6, a thirty-minute daily period is considered desirable. In elementary schools which include the seventh and eighth years, classes are forty to sixty minutes long and are generally given three to five times a week.

When a specialist comes in from outside the school or the regular classroom teacher does not teach the language to his group, a continuous block of time is allotted to language learning during the school day. When the regular classroom teacher also teaches language, the twenty or thirty minutes may be divided into two parts, with some of the instruction taking place before lunch and some before dismissal. This division is generally desirable only in the lower grades, where children's attention span is shorter. Unless flexibility is impossible for administrative reasons, it is wise to let the perceptive teacher decide whether to give the time in one session or in two.

It goes without saying that at the beginning level twenty minutes *every* day is preferable to forty minutes two or three times a week. In the seventh and eighth years—and especially if these constitute the fourth and fifth years of the language program—omitting one day or, if it is absolutely impossible to do otherwise, omitting two days per week but offering a minimum of forty-five minutes per session may be considered.

Over and above everything said here and a recurring theme in any discussion of language learning is the incontrovertible fact that a long, continuous, systematic learning experience produces the best results.

Articulation and Credit Why do people ask questions about language study that they do not think of asking about other areas in the curriculum? Let us ask a few questions of our own. Do we give academic credit for any individual subject in the elementary curriculum? Does every child who leaves the elementary school read English or know mathematics at the sixth-year or the eighth-year level? Does not the good secondary school teacher always have to make provision for groups or individuals in his English or mathematics class, for example, unless students are homogeneously grouped according to previous reading or mathematics grade? Do not problems of articulation exist today between many elementary and secondary schools in areas other than foreign languages?

The question of credit and articulation is the subject of some controversy. None would exist—and we can only hope that the realization of this ideal situation is not in the too distant future—if every elementary school offered a foreign language; if all children succeeded in learning it; if children in the secondary school (junior or senior high school) were able to continue the language they had started in the elementary school. Until that day dawns, several courses may be considered.

Children who have studied a language in the elementary school may be sent to the secondary school in the community which continues the elementary school program and which admits only children who have been in a FLES program. (In small communities which have only one secondary school, this may not be feasible.)

Another solution in a large secondary school would be to have three language tracks: one for FLES "graduates," one for beginners in the same language, and another language for beginners.

Still another answer—to place children in a beginning class of a language they have already studied in the elementary school—may, at first glance, appear harsh or a waste of time. If for some reason inherent in the community, a two-track secondary school program is not possible, why can we not merely consider as extra dividends of the elementary school program the facts that children have developed a liking for language study, acquired a more accurate pronunciation than would have been possible without the early exposure to language, attained an enviable facility with basic language patterns and vocabulary, and gained some desirable social attitudes? All these should be outcomes of an effective elementary school language program.

Children who may be forced to begin language study again need not be made to feel that they are making no progress. The teacher can ask them to participate more quickly in oral reading and role playing. He can ask them to help their schoolmates. He can enlist their assistance in asking questions, in grading papers or homework, or in serving as group leaders of games. (We hasten to add parenthetically that this singling out should not be permitted to affect peer relationships. It should be explained as a procedure which will be of benefit to the entire class.)

Moreover, since reading and writing aspects of language study are initiated or intensified and language structure is studied more systematically at the secondary level, the children will not consider that they are at a standstill. They can be made to feel that they are perfecting their audio-lingual skills and making progress faster in the other basic skills of reading and writing.

Even when—because of circumstances and undesirable as it may be—the child is forced to start *another* language in the secondary schools, he finds that he has an advantage over his classmates. He has learned to identify and produce new sounds and use new muscles; he has learned to express himself in a new way; he has acquired new language habits through intensive repetition; he has learned games and songs which may have parallels in the new second language. A good teacher will show him how to transfer to the new language the skills he acquired in learning the first foreign language.

The alternatives should not be construed as recommendation or condonement of a program which would prevent learners from pursuing a *six-year continuous program* in one language. There is consensus that a six-year period of study, when coupled with the physiological and psychological advantages of an early start, is the minimum time necessary to attain reasonable fluency in the language. The alternatives are offered with some reluctance; administrators, teachers, and community members are urged to explore all avenues for providing the desired continuum.

To summarize: (1) Credit should not be allowed to become a major consideration, because of the recognizable advantages gained by children through a FLES program, and parents and others can be made to realize this; (2) for the children who have not made suitable progress in the FLES program and who are continuing the same language in the junior or senior high school, the secondary school will provide—as it does in mathematics or in English—help in the form of another "track" in the same grade (if numbers warrant this), special grouping within a classroom, or individual remedial work.

The elementary school may recommend that some children drop the language entirely. But might the longer class period in the secondary school (forty-five to sixty minutes as against the twenty or thirty minutes in the elementary school), the use of a textbook, or the more analytical approach to language teaching in the secondary school enable the potential dropout to catch up to his classmates? Might the potential dropout start a *new* language?

In the absence of valid and reliable prognostic instruments, the determination to discontinue a language in the secondary school should be based on an examination of the cumulative school record and a conference with parents. We would also like to recommend, where feasible, that the child be permitted to start another language or to continue the first one. If, after two or three weeks, the new language teacher also feels that the child cannot learn a language, there is still time to transfer him to another subject. Since only one or two children may be involved, such an arrangement can hardly constitute a clerical burden.

Meetings between teachers and administrators of sending and receiving schools can help smooth problems of articulation. Every facet of language teaching—materials, methods, testing—should be explored as often as possible and certainly not less than twice a year. Elementary and secondary school teachers will profit from learning about each other's successes or failures. The real beneficiaries of meetings devoted to articulation will be the children.

The Choice of Language Here again, there is no *one* right answer. In English-speaking communities where there is a large non-English-speaking group, the elementary schools should teach the language of that group. Certainly, too, if several teachers in the school are more familiar with one language than with another, the language chosen should be the one in which the teachers feel most secure. Another aspect to consider is the availability of teacher-training materials or out-of-school personnel.

There is educational justification for the teaching of *any* commonly used language. One of the myths about Americans, for example, is that they can't learn languages or that they find language learning more difficult than do other people. It is totally unfounded. Americans have as good an "ear" as anyone else. If the elementary school program does no more than convince children of that fact so that they will approach the study of languages as adolescents or adults without fear, any cost of teaching languages will have been worthwhile.

In addition to breaking this psychological barrier, there is another advantage to the study of a language—any language. Students gain some knowledge about the nature of language, the methods of learning its sound and structure system, and the importance of habit formation in language learning. They can apply this knowledge to the study of any other language they may be forced to undertake in later years, even if the languages bear little or no relationship to each other.

When a choice can be made, it is always desirable to send a questionnaire to parents indicating language choices. Parents may wish to express some preference because of sentimental or other reasons. If, for any cause, the school cannot offer the language chosen, a note of explanation should be sent to the disappointed parents. Another way of handling this situation would be to state in the original questionnaire the criteria (minimum number of children needed to start a language, for example) which will guide the school or the school district in making a final choice.

Cost of the Program In this program, as in any other, acceptance by parents and by lay leaders of the community is of the utmost importance. In addition to questions related to pupil selection or curriculum crowding, in many communities there will be questions about the cost of the program. In the program proposed here, there are no large additional costs. Classroom teachers or community volunteers do the teaching; tapes are prepared by the neighboring secondary school or college staff or by bilingual volunteers; few books are needed, since reading is not usually begun immediately.

A tape recorder would be useful, as well as a filmstrip and slide projector; phonographs would also be desirable. Nearly all schools already possess such equipment. Tapes and records should be purchased, but certainly, in view of the millions of dollars spent on material in other curriculum areas, no one could possibly object to the minimal cost involved. The use of the language laboratory for elementary school children is still the subject of experimentation and controversy. There can be no question that in the hands of a good teacher and with appropriate materials, the language laboratory can serve as an additional resource in learning. The same statement can be made about any piece of learning equipment ever devised. The fact remains, however, that a most efficacious program is possible without a costly language laboratory installation. Equipment will be discussed in Chapter 5.

Enlisting Community Participation Any expenditure will seem high, however, if the program does not gain widespread acceptance and if the program is not effective. Numerous textbooks discuss methods of winning community acceptance. Only a few suggestions which are particularly applicable to the language program are mentioned here. On the basis of your intimate knowledge of your community you will think of many others. Parents and community leaders may be asked to join in discussions concerning the advisability of introducing languages in the school and will feel part of the program through assisting in (1) selecting a language; (2) preparing some instructional materials (games, pictures, slides or dioramas, charts); (3) making tapes; (4) selecting slides or other visual materials; (5)

locating bilingual speakers; (6) organizing "fiestas" or other schoolwide activities; (7) initiating pen-pal projects; (8) preparing assembly programs; (9) giving talks to pupils on some aspect of the foreign culture; (10) organizing language classes for parents.

Two additional points should be noted: The exclusion of some children in the community from language classes may cause deep friction involving not only the parents of the excluded children but other interested persons. Also, parents like many opportunities to see and hear their children "perform" in the new language.

The heart of the matter, of course, is the effectiveness of the program. Granted the enthusiastic approval and cooperation of the parents and school administrators, it is still the teacher who will bear the major responsibility for carrying out the program. It is the classroom program as parents see it through the eyes of their children which will undergo continuous scrutiny.

Does the teacher need to bring any special knowledge or skills to the task? Does he need to develop any particular attitude? The answer of course is "Yes," and the next chapters are designed to assist teachers of foreign languages in the elementary schools in meeting this new educational challenge of our times.

SUMMARY

Today's national and international commitments, as well as scientific advances of this century, make the knowledge of a second language important to all individuals.

The desirability of introducing foreign languages in the elementary schools can no longer be denied. The emphasis on the development of audio-oral skills based on our knowledge of the nature of language and of language learning necessitates a longer time sequence than has been customary. This same emphasis places a premium on learning a language during childhood when physiological and psychological factors promote the acquisition of the skills involved.

Although administrators may have legitimate reasons for concern, it is the author's belief that (1) all children should study a foreign language; (2) the language introduced should depend, where possible, on the major second language spoken in the community, but primarily on the availability of competent staff; (3) foreign language has as important a place in the curriculum as any other subject area; (4) teachers can be found in school or district staffs, in the community, or at nearby colleges; (5) articulation with the secondary schools is important. Lack of credit need not be a deterrent to a program that should make children appreciate that there are other ways of communicating and that there are people whose customs may be different, but whose values are "as good as" theirs.

A good program is one that (1) starts in the third or fourth grade; (2) integrates the study of language with the other areas of the elementary school curriculum; (3) encourages the classroom teacher to be the language teacher or, if that is impossible, provides for him to remain in the room while his class is learning the language so that the jointly shared experience will become a dynamic, often-referred-to part of the total school day; (4) ensures the unbroken, systematic, and pleasurable study of another language and culture.

Community acceptance and participation are most desirable. The schools should enlist the cooperation of parents and lay leaders in various aspects of the language program. Community acceptance is most easily obtainable if there are evidences of an effective program in which the growth of children in understanding and speaking the language and in understanding the culture of others can be demonstrated. The teacher is the key person. He needs certain skills and attitudes without which the language learning program may be doomed to failure.

2

What Knowledge and Attitudes Should the Teacher Possess?

INTRODUCTION

The teacher is the most vital single factor in the teaching of *any* curriculum area. His role assumes even more importance in the teaching of a foreign language, since—in addition to imparting knowledge and developing new attitudes—he must teach children other physical or physiological skills, i.e., other uses of the muscles or organs they have been using in speaking their native language. Especially with older children, the teacher must overcome difficulties caused by the conflict between the ingrained habits of the native language and the habits required by the new language. He must superimpose new modes of thinking and speaking upon those which have been firmly established since babyhood.

As in any other curriculum area, it is what the teacher does to select and organize the course content and the materials of instruction, to create a friendly environment, to stimulate and maintain interest, to plan varied activities, and to give children a feeling of achievement and success which will determine whether learning will take place. The competent teacher can foster the desire to learn a new mode of communication even in children who have no apparent interest in language study. By the same token, alas, too many children who come to the language class with enthusiasm are soon discouraged by unsympathetic or unskilled teachers.

Any teacher can develop the knowledge, the skills, and the attitudes needed for effective teaching. Although it may be true that some persons are born with a greater predisposition than others for giving of themselves—and that is a basic ingredient in teaching—any person with interest and a willingness to learn can become an excellent teacher. What special knowledge, skills, and attitudes in addition to the knowledge of the foreign language should the foreign language teacher possess or be interested in developing? [1]

Teachers of foreign languages in elementary schools should gain insight into the nature of language. They should study and apply the principles which have been found most effective in teaching language to youngsters. They should be aware of the aims of language teaching in the elementary school program and of their own role in helping to achieve those aims. The dedicated teachers will want to keep abreast of the latest thinking in the language field and will welcome every opportunity to grow in professional knowledge and in linguistic competence. Finally, these teachers will also serve as enthusiastic interpreters of the foreign culture not only for the children in their classes but also for the community at large.

Simple, brief explanations of concepts gleaned from linguistic science, psychology, and anthropology which underlie the teaching and learning of languages follow. Since not all elementary school teachers are or will become language specialists, only definitions and terms which may find immediate application are included. For those teachers who may wish to do further reading, source materials are noted in the Bibliography. The practical procedures which stem from the principles given here will be discussed in detail in Chapters 3, 4, and 5 of this book.

THE NATURE OF LANGUAGE

Stated simply, language is a system of arbitrary, vocal symbols which permits all people in a given culture to *communicate* and to *interact*. Any other person who learns the system can interact and communicate with the native speakers [2] of the language.

---

[1] For the list of criteria prepared by the Modern Language Association, see FL Program Notes later in this book.

[2] "Native speaker" indicates a person born into a language community or one who has learned the language so well that he might be mistaken for a native.

A language, any language, is fundamentally a series of sounds which become meaningful only when they are grouped together in certain definite arrangements. These arrangements have been called "patterns." The arrangement or sequence of words in sentences is usually arbitrary. In English, for example, we can say, "I see him," but we cannot say, "Him I see," or "See I him." Within the pattern, arbitrarily established by the system of the particular language, however, speakers can substitute other words, provided they fit into the same slot or groove; e.g., "I know her" or "He knows her" is the same pattern as "We see him."

The forms of words are also arbitrarily set by the language. For example, in English we say "boy" to mean one boy, "boys" to mean more than one. We say "I know" to mean a general truth or the present time, "I knew" to indicate the past.

The words themselves are arbitrary *symbols* for concepts. They are symbols which are generally understood by all the speakers of the language. The sounds "pencil" stand for something we use for writing. No native speaker would have a vision of bread, for example, when he heard "pencil."

In normal communication, the native speaker is not conscious of the form of the words he uses or of the order in which he places them. He is conscious only of the idea he is trying to express.

Language is *learned behavior*. The infant learns the language of the community in which he is born by constant reinforcement and by the reactions of those around him to the sounds he makes. For example, a child learns to say "water" or "bread" or anything else when his production of certain sounds brings him water or bread each time. The satisfaction of his desire for bread or water is usually accompanied by a family member's reinforcing statement, such as "Baby wants bread (water)" or "Do you want bread?"

Linguists consider the *spoken* form of the language primary for several reasons. We note three here: (1) Children learn to understand and speak their native language for several years *before* they learn to read and write it—if they learn to read and write at all; (2) although *all* normal human beings can understand and speak, many cannot read and write; (3) writing is a secondary system derived only from what people say. Writing is often called "a symbolization of a symbolization" since the symbols (the letters of the alphabet in English, for example) used in writing "represent" the words of the language. These words are themselves symbols, names, or meanings which all speakers of the same language attach to the same objects or concepts. As one well-known writer remarked, "No one in a language community can call a flower a rose today and a turnip tomorrow and be understood."

Language is the central feature of the culture of any community. It is a reflection of the thoughts, the feelings, the values, and the experiences of a community of speakers. It is their expression of the way in which they view the total content—physical, spiritual, and moral—of their environment.

If we accept these basic assumptions about language and culture which linguistic scientists and anthropologists make, we must accept the principles of learning which are derived from them. Under principles we also include, however, the psychological laws that give us insight into such important teaching factors as motivation, habit formation, reward, and success. We must add, too, our knowledge of the characteristics of children at various age levels. Nor in discussing teaching in the elementary schools can we ignore the philosophy which permeates all the areas of elementary school life.

Before stating the essential learning principles from which our teaching methods evolve, let us turn our attention to the aims of language teaching in the elementary schools. What can we hope to accomplish?

GOALS OF LANGUAGE LEARNING IN THE ELEMENTARY SCHOOLS

Childhood, as the literature indicates, is considered the most favorable period for laying a solid foundation for oral fluency. It is also the formative period in which nascent prejudices can be eradicated. Therefore the elementary school program should strive toward achievement in two major areas—linguistic and cultural.

Children should learn to understand and to speak the foreign language with reasonable accuracy and fluency in the situations within which and about which children of their age group normally speak. They should learn to appreciate that there are other ways of communicating and that another language permits them to express the same ideas, the same likes and dislikes, the same needs and desires as well as their native tongue. This concept of the richness of other modes of communication is important if we are to overcome the provincial feeling held by many that only in one's own language can one conduct an intelligent conversation or discussion.

The elementary school program should also develop in children the ability to read and write what they have learned to say. The degree to which the reading and writing skills are developed will vary from community to community. All communities, however, should initiate reading and writing activities after a reasonable period of purely audio-oral activity. This statement will be expanded below.

If the program helps a child develop confidence in his ability to speak and to read another language, he will undertake the study of a second or a third foreign language in later life without fear or reluctance. Moreover, where the teacher points out the "transfer" (as in possible cognates) the child's competency in English can be enhanced through the use of materials learned in the foreign language. Such transfer is not usually automatic; it should be consciously "written into" the program if the foreign language lends itself to this approach.

The good foundation of oral fluency which FLES makes possible carries with it several concomitant outcomes, which become more apparent over the years: (1) Deep personal satisfaction is gained from the knowledge of having acceptable and praiseworthy pronunciation not only at succeeding school levels but also in later-life contacts with speakers of the language; (2) the possibility of enjoyment of the literature of the language in the original is increased, so that colleges may well be able to devote their efforts to presenting literature rather than pronunciation, grammar, or remedial work; (3) personality enrichment and even character development are possible results of the ability to grasp the language nuances in great literature and to understand foreign language broadcasts; and (4) last, communication with non-English-speaking persons who may be living in the community or, if one lives abroad, with the native speakers of the language one may have learned is possible.

With relation to the second objective—cultural understanding—a good program should underscore the facts that people all over the world are basically similar. All have the same needs, wants, and desires.[3] Some customs may be different because of geographical or his-

---

[3] For an interesting and informative discussion of this concept, see Clyde Kluckhohn, *Mirror for Man,* Fawcett Publications, Inc., Greenwich, Conn., V, pp. 26–27.

torical factors. The differences, however, should not be exaggerated to mean that one culture is better than or inferior to any other. The foreign language elementary school program should not only lend support to this concept which other subject areas—social studies and science, for example—try to inculcate but also make unique and positive contributions. Through activities which will be outlined in Chapter 4, the foreign language program can help sensitize children to the values of other cultures. It can lead them to accept differences among peoples with respect and understanding. It can foster attitudes which will prevent their outright rejection of another way of life because it does not parallel their own.

PRINCIPLES OF LANGUAGE LEARNING

Findings of linguistic science and current concepts of "culture," as well as psychological laws of learning, should form the basis of a sound learning program.

Principles Derived from Linguistic Science Some principles derived from linguistic science which affect the role of teachers may be stated as follows:

- The sounds of the language should receive priority—not sounds in isolation, but sounds in authentic expressions and sentences spoken with the intonation and rhythm which would be used by a native speaker.
- Learners should be shown, through numerous examples, what the "system" of the new language is and how it operates. They must acquire the language signals or "code"—the sound system, the grammar, and the vocabulary—which will permit them to engage in communication.
- Since language is a complex system involving forms and arrangements of words and problems of form and word order are usually stumbling blocks to real communication, matters of form and word order should be made habitual and automatic through constant repetition and reintroduction.
- At this level, the *habitual* use of the most frequently used patterns and items of language should take precedence over the mere accumulation of words. The acquisition of vocabulary should be a subsidiary goal at the beginning stage. Vocabulary will increase rapidly when reading is begun.

- Vocabulary should be taught and practiced only in the context of real situations so that meaning will be clarified and reinforced.
- Classroom activities should center about authentic speech situations—dialogues, interchanges ("I'm fourteen. How old are you?"), descriptions, rejoinders ("Are you ready?" "Of course.")—where two or more children are involved.
- Dialogues and other materials should not contain *simplified* language. They should be short and authentic, however, and should conform to other criteria which we will indicate below.
- The teacher or a native voice on tape should give the model for all utterances.[4] Students should not be expected to say anything which they have not heard *repeatedly* at normal speed and with normal intonation. Speech should not be slowed down nor rhythm distorted because of the mistaken idea that it will increase understanding.
- New patterns of language should be introduced and practiced with vocabulary that students already know. For example, if we were teaching the interrogative form, "Do you have _____?" the point of departure would be a sentence the children already know, e.g., "I have a dog at home."
- Very little new material should be introduced in any one lesson. New material should always be combined with previously taught language items in varied activities, e.g., playing a game. The same expressions or sentences should be used with different cultural topics. As quickly as possible, children should be made aware of the fact that the same words or the same patterns can serve many purposes—as is true in English.
- Learning a language means forming new habits through intensive practice in hearing and speaking. The emphasis should always be on language in actual use. Rules of grammar or language analysis should be omitted entirely at this stage, particularly if grammar is not being taught in the English language arts program. Descriptive statements, however, e.g., "Words such as _____ and _____ come at the (end) of the sentence," are not only permissible but often welcomed by older children. It is desirable that children be given insight into the regularity or general truth of such statements through hear-

---

[14] The two-word phrase *utterance unit* will mean any stretch of speech "by one person before which there was silence on his part and after which there was also silence on his part." Charles Fries, *The Structure of English,* Harcourt, Brace and Company, Inc., New York, 1952, p. 23.

ing, saying, and later seeing many examples which include the same grammatical item.

- Previously taught vocabulary and structures should be reintroduced in subsequent units whenever logical or possible. The "spiral" approach to language learning, which provides for the continuous recurrence of the same materials, always in greater depth, is explained more fully below.
- Communication implies hearing and speaking, listening to and carrying out directions, listening to and making statements, listening to and answering questions, making rejoinders, e.g., "Why?" "Certainly." Students should have extensive practice as listeners and speakers in authentic situations in which they would normally take part in their native tongue.
- English should be used sparingly and judiciously in the classroom. Until children have accumulated enough vocabulary so that the teacher can make himself understood through paraphrases and other devices, however, some explanations will have to be given in English. It is important, however, that the children do not use English in the classroom. The place of translation is discussed in Chapter 4.
- Because of the recognition that speech is primary, that understanding and speaking are the skills most needed today, and that understanding and speaking speed up the reading process, the sequence of language learning skills is (1) understanding, (2) speaking, (3) reading and writing.
- In general, reading should not be introduced until children have a good knowledge of the sound system and the most frequently used structures. When reading is begun, the initial materials should be drawn from the conversations, stories, or dialogues which children have learned or memorized. In this way, reading will constitute a visual *recall* of familiar spoken material. The time that should elapse between beginning to learn a language and the introduction of reading will be discussed later in Chapter 4.
- Writing should be introduced after reading. Initial writing exercises should consist of copying familiar patterns, dialogues, conversations, or reading passages. Improvisation should be discouraged until basic patterns are firmly established.

Principles Derived from Psychological Sciences Let us turn our attention now to some psychological laws which should guide our thinking and planning:

- Language learning is a complex process demanding the acquisition of many skills. The extent to which these skills are acquired depends upon such factors as concentration of attention on each of the components of the skill; the repeated practice of each of the components; the insight the child acquires into the relationship which exists among the various facets of the skill; and his understanding of the relationship of each skill to the total act of communication.

Techniques of skill development will be discussed in the following chapters, but let us examine a brief example now. In teaching children to speak, for example, we would have to make sure they could (1) hear and produce the sounds of the language; (2) put the sounds together with correct stress, rhythm, pauses, and intonation; (3) use word forms which signal the meaning they wished to convey; (4) place words in their proper slots in the sentence or utterance; (5) know the vocabulary item for the concept being expressed; (6) respond appropriately to the previous speaker or to the previous stimulus (Was an action, a rejoinder, or another question called for?); (7) use the signals required by the culture (e.g., in French, "tu" or "vous" as the familiar or the polite form of the pronoun "you").

- Motivation and incentive are necessary for successful performance. Successful performance and subsequent reward heighten motivation and incentive. The environment and the activities of the language classroom should increase the learners' motivation and should provide them with intensive but pleasurable practice in listening to and speaking the language.

- The classroom activities should strengthen the language skills and should not be problem-solving exercises. The techniques used by the teacher in aural-oral work should encourage the highest rate of *correct* responses, thus giving children a feeling of success, achievement, and security.

- When corrections are made, they should be made immediately, but in ways which will bring about learning and not frustration or discouragement (see Chapter 4).

- Language should be practiced in normal everyday situations with which children can easily identify.

- Frequent review and reentry of the same material—at increasingly longer intervals—is necessary for retention.

- In reviewing, variations in or logical combinations of familiar materials should be introduced and practiced. Such variation changes the pace of the lesson and retains (or recaptures) the interest of the children.

• The children—their environment and their experiences—should be the starting point of any lesson. The first association with a new concept or language item should be one that the children can grasp because it is something within *their* experience. Children should be helped to recall something familiar which is related to or contrasts with a new item to be learned.

Principles Derived from Anthropological (or Social) Sciences This last point brings us to a teaching application of the concept of culture as it is defined today. Since language is the central feature of a culture, children learn to appreciate the customs, values, and mores of children in other countries by saying what the "foreign children" would say in talking about their school days, holidays, songs, dances, or foods. Through carrying out such activities as plays, dramatizations, storytelling, pen-pal writing, creative art work, or even doing problems in mathematics in the foreign language, children can be made aware of activities of children of their own age in the foreign country—children who also go to school and do mathematics, have birthdays, name days, or school holidays.

Children should be taught to say and do (with gestures and facial expressions) what children of the same age would say or do in similar situations in the foreign land. Such learning is of far greater value than the mere repetition of dates or of names of rivers or famous men.

THE TEACHER'S ROLE

Our present insight into the nature of language and the resultant principles of language learning have brought about changes in the role of the classroom teacher in the language class, particularly in the *beginning* language class. Although no one would deny that it is most desirable for the teacher to have a fluent knowledge of the language, he can still be an effective teacher at this level with a more limited knowledge of the language. Since improvisation by either teacher or children is discouraged in the early stages, since only a limited number of structures and vocabulary items are taught—and these in small doses—and since the teacher's major task is to establish new habits of language, he should *master* the few language items he will need and learn how to use them and teach them in every possible cultural situation. As quickly as feasible, of course, the teacher will want to grow in language competency through one or more of the resources available to him. Until the teacher shortage is overcome, however, the role of the nonspecialist classroom teacher may be defined as follows:

1. He should plan his language lessons with great care. For example, the language items for emphasis should be judiciously selected; the activities and instructional materials for introducing and practicing the new items should be interestingly arranged; language items previously learned should be kept alive through constant use where logical; provision should be made not only for the intensive pattern practice leading to habit formation but also for the practice of the normal forms of conversation in real situations.

2. He should make certain that he is missing no opportunity to correlate the foreign language with the other curriculum areas which he is teaching.

3. He should provide for the continuous reintroduction of the language material he has taught. The reintroduction can be within the cultural topic used in the initial presentation or in others where the language item fits logically.

4. He should use the new language in any everyday situation where its use would be normal. For example, he should greet the children, call the roll, dismiss the class, ask for the date or the weather in the foreign language.

5. He should give practice—intensive, but varied—so that the new language habits will become firmly fixed. He must strike a happy balance between maintaining the children's interest and forming new habits.

6. He should make use of English in the language classroom sparingly, but he should not hesitate to use it to clarify instructions or to make repetition meaningful to the children.

7. He should learn how to use choral and group-recitation procedures in order to give as many children as possible the opportunity to recite at one time.

8. Even though he may be a language learner too, he should keep the ratio of teacher-pupil speaking to about 20 : 80. The children will definitely continue their language study and will need the intensive practice while he may not.

9. He should learn to detect children's pronunciation errors and make every effort to correct them.

10. He should furnish the model over and over again for the new material being taught or make provision for the tape or the language record to do so.

11. If he works with a language specialist and if the program can be so arranged, the classroom teacher should remain in the room while the specialist is teaching the language. The reasons for this should be obvious on the basis of everything that has been said.

SOURCES OF HELP

The classroom teacher who is not a language specialist but who would like to participate in today's exciting language teaching program can get help from many sources. Some literature in the field—textbooks, guides, and professional journals—is listed in Sources and Resources for Teachers. An examination of these will help him learn what has been done, what experimentation is being conducted in the field, what new training programs and scholarships are being offered by government agencies, universities, or foundations and who is eligible for them. Keeping abreast of advances in one's field is essential in any subject area.

In addition to studying the available literature, teachers may wish to attend language institutes and seminars sponsored by government agencies or by local colleges. Commercial television programs and radio broadcasts in the foreign language are often available. Teacher-oriented television programs may also be part of a broader project of in-service training of which teachers should become aware.

There are many other official or semiofficial opportunities for teachers to perfect their knowledge of a foreign language, to acquire a new language, to gain insight into a foreign culture, and to learn ways of teaching a language and culture. There are foreign exchange programs for study or teaching. There are always courses at the universities and in evening secondary or adult education schools. There are also bilingual persons in the community.

There is also available to teachers a wealth of records and tapes on the commercial market which permit immersion in a foreign language. Although these may not give the exact phrases and words the learner may be called upon to teach, attentive listening to sounds of the language and sound sequences in authentic sentences cannot help but increase the teacher's linguistic competency.

SOME INTANGIBLES

The willingness to develop professionally, the enthusiasm for teaching, and the love for children which are the hallmarks of teachers of any subject anywhere should also characterize the language teacher. Because of the nature of his subject, however, and because the value of FLES is not universally accepted, the teacher of foreign language should also possess other attributes.

He should bend every effort to grow in his knowledge of the language and other facets of the culture of which the language is the central feature. He should be a sympathetic but objective interpreter of the culture for the school and the community, as well as for his pupils.

He should breathe life into the foreign language program so that the enthusiasm of his pupils for language study will be transmitted to their parents and the community. He should be willing to plan many culminating activities, such as plays and festivals, to which parents and others can be invited.

Finally, he should be deeply cognizant of the unprecedented role he is playing in the development of international understanding and of the increased responsibilities which are the concomitants of his role.

SUMMARY

In addition to the knowledge, skills, and attitudes which all teachers need and in addition to a command of the foreign language, the teacher of foreign language should possess insight into the nature of language and the principles of language learning which stem from many sources —linguistic science, psychology, and anthropology. It is important that the teacher believe that language is primarily a spoken vehicle of communication and that the acquisition of a language depends upon the formation of new habits.

It is essential, too, that he recognize that these new insights alter the traditional role of the language teacher. The teacher helps children understand and say a limited number of language items. He creates situations in the classroom so that children receive extensive and pleasurable practice, which helps make the use of the language habitual and natural. He gives practice in forms of speaking—dialogues, for example—that people normally use. He initiates reading and writing activities only after children have a reasonably good command of aural-oral skills.

Since language and culture are closely interwoven, the teacher and children engage in many experiences which will help the children appreciate the basic oneness of all human beings, while making them aware of both the similarities and the differences in specific customs or mores.

3

What Should Be Taught?

INTRODUCTION

If children are to grow in their awareness of the foreign language as "another way" to communicate, they must be given many opportunities to use the new language to express the same feelings, enthusiasms, preferences, thoughts, or desires that they are capable of expressing in their native tongue. For young children, language assumes meaning when it is associated with things they can hear, touch, or see. It becomes even more meaningful when it is linked with a situation in which they themselves play an important role. In the first school stage, their world usually revolves around their immediate environment, both at home and in school. As they get older, this limited world is expanded by excursions, both real and imaginary, into the wider community. Soon the wider community may embrace other peoples and countries.

The curriculum in all areas of the elementary school takes into account the progressive growth of children's ability to perceive and appreciate people and things beyond their immediate environment. Since the foreign language curriculum is part of the total elementary school program, enriching it and being enriched in turn, it must also take into consideration the stages in the development of children.

What language items will young children need in order to talk about their immediate environment, both in and out of school?

The words and sentence patterns used in talking in the native tongue about daily activities at home and in school differ at various stages in children's development. They also differ in accordance with differing home backgrounds and community resources. Some children come to school with large vocabularies and rich backgrounds of experiences; others express themselves in short, simple sentences with an extremely limited vocabulary.

As they are given verbal and nonverbal experiences in school, children gain the ability to talk about the same situation or activity in more complex sentences; they develop a more exact or colorful vocabulary. It seems logical, therefore, in considering language items for inclusion in a FLES curriculum, that we be guided by our knowledge of the diverse factors which are normal in the pattern of growth and development of children.

The awareness of developmental stages of growth has given rise to a method or principle of learning which has been termed "spiral." Stated simply, a spiral approach is one in which the same topic—the classroom, for example—may be discussed at the beginning level and at any level thereafter. The words and expressions used to discuss the same item or area of classroom or community living will differ at each succeeding level. At the beginning, for example, the talk about a pencil might be "Do you have your pencil?" or something simpler, such as "This is a pencil." The second stage might include "I forgot my pencil today." The third might be "I have to go to the stationery store to buy a pencil this afternoon." Thus in each wider circle—which coincides, of course, with the growing maturity of the children—the sentences are longer and more complex; the vocabulary is both more varied and more precise; relationships between objects, people, or cause and effect are also expressed.

This concept will be treated more fully in the second half of this chapter, where possible areas of integration between language items and topics of interest to children will be suggested.

SELECTING THE MATERIAL

Language presupposes two or more people talking together. The talk may revolve about something which is taking place at the moment, has already taken place, or will take place. What do people usually talk about? More specifically, what do children anywhere talk about? The normal topics of their discourse should determine the "cultural" [1]

---

[1] "Culture" is used in the anthropological sense here and throughout this book.

themes or "centers of interest" around and through which we should teach them the new language.

In a real act of communication, the situation or setting, the language, and the cultural themes are integrated. When one child meets another in the corridor (setting) and says (using the sounds, grammatical patterns, and words of the language), "Let's have lunch at noon" ("lunch at noon" with someone being part of the culture), neither speaker nor listener stops to think of setting, language, or cultural concept as a separate or distinct entity. The three are intimately blended together without awareness. It is this merging together of language and cultural concept—perhaps for eventual use in a foreign situation—which should be the culminating objective of language teaching.

Helping pupils attain the ability to blend language elements into normal communication requires careful selection of material and skillful planning. For convenience in curriculum construction, the cultural topics and the language items for the entire elementary school program are listed separately below. Possible means of integrating language items and cultural topics at various learning levels are suggested. The lists, as you will note, are not exhaustive nor prescriptive.

If the knowledge of any other language item or cultural topic seems important in your school because of the environment, the textbooks, or special interests of children or community members, insert it in the list. If these same factors make omission of any topic desirable, do not hesitate to eliminate it.

The placement of topics in categories is purely arbitrary. For example, expressions of time, dates, or shopping might have been placed under a topic heading called "Numbers." The sequence of items in specific categories is not so important as the principle of reintroducing the same items in increasingly complex sentence patterns and in cultural situations where they fit logically.

Experience has shown that it is not essential to maintain a rigid sequence in introducing new language items, *if*—and this is the crux of the matter—provision has been made to teach the new item in relation to something the children know in English or have learned in the foreign language. Sequence of learning will be discussed again later in this chapter.

Since it is hoped that this book will be useful to FLES teachers of all foreign languages and that the number of languages offered in the elementary schools will continue to increase, language items are given in English only. (In Sample Materials illustrations are culled from several languages.) It is expected that teachers, when presenting cultural topics, will point out similarities or differences between the children's cultural pattern and that of the foreign country, e.g., "French children do *not* go to school on Thursday. They go to school on Saturday."

CULTURAL TOPICS [2]

Greetings and leave-takings at various hours of the day—used with peers, members of the family, teachers, older persons

Expressions of courtesy—used with peers, members of the family, teachers, strangers

Classroom routines—attendance, lateness, dismissals, removing or putting on clothing, distributing or putting away material; requests by the teacher to deliver a message, go to the blackboard, stand, sit, put away materials, get clothing, etc.; preparation for the snack period or other class activities

Identification—Names of children

    Words for father, mother, brother, sister, relatives

    Names of immediate family members and relatives

    Address; name of city, state, country

    Age

    Names of children sitting nearby

    Names of friends

    Names of people in the school (principal, nurse, custodian, clerks, etc.)

    Descriptions of people

The School

Classroom (things in it, the program, the activities)

People and their duties (librarian, nurse, doctor, principal, etc.)

Building and locations of special rooms (gymnasium, office, library, lunchroom, etc.)

Activities (plays and programs in the auditorium, trips, exhibits, graduation, parent participation, elections, parties, clubs, the newspaper)

[2] Each topic may be expanded further. Only a few of the possibilities are given for each topic.

Guidance activities such as choice of junior or senior high school and future career plans

The Home

Rooms and furnishings

Activities and related materials (cleaning, cooking, eating, dressing, studying, reading, listening to the radio, looking at television, receiving company, entertaining, fixing or making things)

Duties of various family members (cleaning, shopping)

Pets (names, care, play)

Hobbies

Toys

Indoor recreation

Food

Meals [3] (breakfast, lunch, dinner or supper), time and names of meals, kinds of food served

Shopping (food stores and employees, cost of food, containers and packaging, weights, money)

Preparation

Recipes (typical dishes)

Table settings

Table manners and formulas of courtesy

Special holiday menus in the children's country and in the foreign country (e.g., New Year's Day)

Health

Parts of the body

Personal cleanliness (daily routines, prevention of illness)

Illness (names, symptoms, special foods, medicines)

Visits to doctor or dentist

Hospitals and clinics

The drugstore

[3] It is desirable to be sensitive to your community in treating the food or any other topic. For example, do not extol a breakfast of orange juice, bacon, and eggs, etc., if you are teaching in a community whose economy or culture would not make such a breakfast typical. Nothing prevents you, however, from teaching the *names* of foods and having them used in many different ways, e.g., "I don't like orange juice," "I never drink orange juice," "Mr. _____ prefers bacon and eggs."

Clothing

Names of garments (boys', girls', dolls', parents', babies')
Seasonal changes
Materials, colors, sizes
Care at home and outside (dry cleaning)
Shopping (money, likes and dislikes, packaging, department and neighborhood stores, mail order)

Recreation

At home (visiting, television, radio, record playing, reading)
In the community (movies, clubs, parks, zoos, museums, library, theater)
Sports (neighborhood and community, seasonal sports, camps and camping, active and spectator sports)
Games (language, mechanical, scientific)
Hobbies (stamp collecting, drawing)
Parties (types, invitations, presents, activities)
Songs and dances

Holidays

In your country and abroad
Dates and kinds (weekend, summer, national, religious)
Customs (cards, presents, food)

The Community—Rural or Urban

Services (post office, hospital, firehouse, etc.)
Stores (dry cleaner, shoe repair, barber shop, beauty parlor, etc.)
Shopping
Recreation facilities (park, zoo, museums, community centers)
Places of interest (statues, homes of famous people)
Means of transportation (bus, car, train, bicycle, taxi)
Eating places (restaurants, cafeterias, drugstores, ice cream parlors)
Communication (telephone, mail services)

The Wider Community—Traveling Abroad

Work

Parents
Other family members

Community helpers
Children (at home and outside)

Other Topics

Names of boys and girls
The weather, the seasons, and the months
Numbers (cardinal and ordinal)
Time and dates
Money
Map study and directions
Plans for a trip to the country where the language is spoken
People of current or historical interest
Learnings from music, art, social studies, nature study, and any other curriculum area of interest to the children and within their ability to discuss

LANGUAGE ITEMS FOR INTENSIVE PRACTICE

These include formulas, courtesy expressions, rejoinders, exclamations:

> Good morning (afternoon, evening).
> Hello.
> Good-by.
> So long.
> I'll see you again.
> I'll see you soon.
> Give my regards to _____.
> How are you?
> Fine, thank you, and you?
> So-so.
> Thank you.
> You're welcome.
> How do you do?
> I'm glad to meet you.
> May I _____?
> Certainly.
> Why, of course.
> Have a good time.
> Good luck.
> Congratulations.

I'm sorry.
Pardon me.
I beg your pardon.
That's all right.
What's the matter?
Happy birthday.
Many returns of the day.
Please.
Not at all.
Really?
Isn't that so? (Don't you think so?)
Dr., Judge, Father, Rabbi [and other titles]
Happy holiday.
Merry Christmas.
Happy New Year.
Welcome.
Gosh!

Some classroom expressions that should be practiced intensively are:

Present.
He (she's) absent.
Please stand.
Please sit.
Open your (books).[4]
Close your (books).
Count.
Take out your (pens).
Take off your (coat).
Put on your (hat).
Put away your (paints).
Go to the (board).
Point to (the flag).
Let's (sing).
Let's (learn).
Let's play (the game).
Let's line up.

[4] Parentheses around words in this and subsequent lists mean that other similar words may be used in this same position.

It's time for (lunch).
Pass the (paper).
Touch (the picture).
Listen.
Say.
All together.
(Boys) in this row.
(Girls) in group (one).
Show (us) the (picture).
(Show) (me) your (tongue). [or other expressions used in health inspection]
Repeat after (me).
Answer.
Ask (him) the question.
Raise your hand.
Slowly.
Quickly.
Louder, please.

Some basic structures that should be emphasized are:

My name is _____.
What's (your) name?
It's _____.
What's your (father's) name?
What's this?
What's that?
What are these?
What are those?
This is a _____.
That's a _____.
These are _____.
Those are _____.
It's a _____.
They're _____.
Is this a _____?
Is that a _____?
No, it's not a _____.
Where is the _____?
Where are the _____?

It's (on) (under) the (chair).
They're (near) (next to) the (table).
There is a (book) on the (table).
There are (two) (pens) on the (desk).
(I'm) a (pupil).
(Are) (you) a (pupil)?
Yes, (I'm) a (pupil).
No, (I'm) not a (pupil).
(I) (have) a (pencil).
(Do you have) (a) (pencil)?
No, (I don't have) (a) (pencil).
Where (do you) live?
(I live) in (Washington).
(I live) at (22) (Maple) (Street).
(I) (need) (a) (book).
(I) (don't) need (a) (pencil).
(Do) (you) (want) (the) (crayon)?
(Do) (you) (want) (the) (red) (crayon)?
(I) (have) (my) (hat).
How old (are) (you)?
(I'm) _____ years old.
Where is (he)?
Who is (he)?
How is (he)?
What is (he)?
What time is it?
It's (four) o'clock.
It's (noon).
It's (half) past (two).
It's (ten) (to) (three).
It's a quarter (to) (three).
How (are) (you)?
(I'm) (fine).
How's the weather?
It's (fine).
It's (raining).
It's (cold) in (winter).
(I) (have) a (red) (hat).
(He) is a (big) (boy).

What (are you) doing?
(I'm) (walking).
What's (today)?
What's (today's) date?
It's the (twentieth) of (August).
What (do) (you) do every (morning)?
I (get up).
What time do you (get up)?
What time do you (usually) (go to bed)?
(I get up) at (eight) o'clock.
(How many) (books) (do you) have?
(I have) (three) (books).
When is (your) birthday?
(My) birthday is on (August) (twenty-sixth).
It's on (August) (twenty-sixth).
How much (is) (the) (pencil)?
How much (is) (it)?
(It's) (four) (cents).
(I) (know) (him).
(I) (went) (there) last (year).
Where is (your) (house)?
It's (near) (here).
It's (far from) the (school).
(I'll) (see) (you) (there) (tomorrow).
(Whose) (book) is (this)?
It's (mine).
(Whose) (books) are (these)?
They're (mine).
(My) (dog) is (smarter) than your dog.
(My) (dog) is the (smartest).
(Mine) is the (smartest).
(I have) (a lot of) (money).
(I don't have) (any) (money).
(Do you have) (any) (money)?
(I) have (a few) (books).
Do you want (some) (ice cream)?
Would (you) like (some) (cake)?
(I) used to (go) there.
(I) (don't) go there (anymore).

(I) can't (go).
(Give) (him) (the) (book).
(I) like the dog.
(I) like to (swim).
(I'm) (thirsty).
(I) have a (headache).
(Go) to the (door).
Don't (go) to the (door).
Let's (go) to the (movies).
(Have you) ever (gone) to the (movies)?
(I've) (never) (gone).
How long (have) (you) been (waiting)?
(I've) been (waiting) for (an hour).
(Speak) (slowly).
(I'll) (go) if (you) (go).
(I'd) (go) if you (went).
(Which) (book) do you (want)?
Give (me) (that) one.
(You're) a (teacher), (aren't you)?
May (I) (go) (there)?
(I) (must) (go).
(I'm) (sorry) (I) (have to) (go).

OTHER VOCABULARY ITEMS

Vocabulary can be divided into two major categories: function words and content words. Under function words we place such "little" words as prepositions ("to," "for," "by"), demonstrative words ("this," "that"), question words ("who," "how"), and "auxiliary" verbs ("be," "have to," "must," "should"). Function words have no meaning by themselves, but they are of primary importance. Some of the important function words were included naturally in the preceding list of basic structures.

There are very few functions words in a language, whereas the number of content words—words for things, actions, and qualities—is virtually limitless. No list of content words will be given here, nor should any such list be used exactly as found in any other source. The selection of content words will depend on the grade in which language is introduced; the resources, sites, and location of the community (rural or urban, for example); the background of experiences of the children;

the approach selected to teach the structure of the language; the cultural topic within which the basic language structures are taught.

A number of considerations should be borne in mind in relation to vocabulary:

1. Acquisition of an extensive vocabulary is *not* the primary aim of language learning in the elementary grades. The children's store of content words will increase rapidly when reading begins. A good knowledge of the sounds and arrangements of a limited number of words in various kinds of sentences or utterances should be our chief concern at this level. The objective should be to help children use a limited vocabulary and a limited set of structures accurately and confidently in natural situations. The function words within the structures are practiced and learned automatically, since structures would not exist without function words.

2. Reintroduction of the same vocabulary with different structures and in different cultural topics is more desirable than burdening children with a large vocabulary load. Their immediate need is to learn the new sound and structure systems of the language.

3. Not all the vocabulary associated with a center of interest or cultural topic should be given in any one grade. For example, in learning about family members, children would be taught to talk about their parents, brothers, and sisters in the first year. In the following year, they could talk about their grandparents; in the next, about their uncles, aunts, and cousins.

4. Children should be given the vocabulary they need, however, to make the situations they are talking about sound normal and natural to them.

5. Some vocabulary items used in dialogues, in classroom expressions, and even in formulas will remain a part of the children's *passive* or *recognitional vocabulary* for weeks or months and possibly throughout the elementary program. Even in the native language, the *active* vocabulary (for speaking and writing) is smaller than the listening or reading vocabulary.

6. No definite figure can be cited as the number of active words children should learn. In general, a group of three to five new words in each lesson in the first year is recommended, with the number increasing at each level.

7. "Three to five new words" mean those singled out for emphasis in practice exercises or language activities and used in building new

sentences on known patterns or structures. Let us take a new word, "hospital." If the children know how to say "I went to the store," they can form a new sentence, "I went to the hospital" or "He (she) went to the hospital" on the known pattern. In addition, they should be helped to use the new active words in any skill (listening, speaking, reading, or writing) or communication activity where they logically belong.

8. Dialogues, even beginning ones, may contain many additional words which children will learn and use as listeners and speakers. They are often inserted to give dialogues a natural, authentic flavor, and they may or may not become a source of intensive active practice later in the same grade or even within the elementary school program.

On the other hand, it is suggested that in writing dialogues even the passive words be those which are known to be of high frequency and general use in the foreign language. In English, for example, people say, "I feel very tired," rather than "I feel extreme fatigue." "Soup" is a higher-frequency word than "cheese soufflé."

9. One of the principal criteria in vocabulary selection is the authenticity of the language. The question should always be: Is this what a foreign child would say?

10. Another essential basis for vocabulary selection is the *normal, immediate* use to which the new words can be put. If the children need the word "cow" to talk about the animal which is always a few feet from their classroom door, the teaching of the word "cow" would precede the teaching of the word "ship," for example, since the ship may be two thousand miles away.

If the class looks out on skyscrapers, the word "skyscraper" would receive priority, since it would be useful in talking about a neighborhood trip or answering a question such as "What do you see from the window?"

11. At the beginning levels, it is also desirable to present words which can be pictured or demonstrated easily. This minimizes the need for giving English equivalents. Later, familiar words in the foreign language can be used in explaining abstract or nondemonstrable concepts and nonpicturable words.

12. A heavier load of vocabulary items may be given in the first few lessons, until children accumulate enough vocabulary and structures to talk with meaning and pleasure. Eagerness to learn the new language will make children accept and learn a larger vocabulary with

enthusiasm. Their large stock of words will enable them to talk about more people and things and will in itself engender further interest.

ORGANIZING THE COURSE CONTENT

Grading the Structures Although a systematic presentation of the course content should be carefully planned, no *single* approach or authority should dictate the exact order of presentation of cultural situations, structures, or vocabulary. Many approaches are possible and even desirable.

Some authorities are of the opinion that the choice of a cultural situation—a holiday or shopping, for example—should determine the structures and the vocabulary to be used. Others think that it is more desirable to grade the language items to be taught and then build cultural situations around them.

Either approach could be effective, provided the principles of language learning discussed above are not lost sight of in the planning. One of the questions we should ask in grading structures is: Are we basing this new knowledge on something the children already know either in their native tongue or in the foreign language? It does not really matter if after teaching "My name is _____," we teach "His (her) name is _____" (talking about the child in the next seat) or "I live in _____." If we think these structures are important—and of course they are—we should make provision to teach them *at some time* during the three- or four-year course. The time will depend on the children's need to use the structure in an interesting activity (game, play, or dramatization); on what has preceded; on what will follow; and on some other factors we will now consider.

Another question in "ordering" the structures should be: Will we be able to use this language pattern in many situations? For example, "What's this?" "This is a _____," and "It's a _____," would be highly serviceable patterns, since they can be used to introduce and practice many content words.

Structures which contrast most sharply with English might be taught early to older children, who may be starting language study in the fifth or sixth grade. (The bilingual specialist should be consulted in selecting these contrasting items.) If contrasting structures are introduced early and their frequent, systematic reuse provided for throughout the program, the children will have many opportunities for repetition over several years. It is only by dint of such repetition that the use of a language item will become normal and habitual. (Notice the qualifying phrase "with older children." Generally, younger children do not analyze or recognize "contrasts." One item is usually as easy as another for them.)

Since language learning is cumulative and since the important structures cannot all be presented at once, it is necessary to formulate an overall list of language items and to determine which item needs to be taught before another and which might logically follow. For example, a pattern such as "No, I don't" would be illogical unless we had taught another pattern such as "Do you like pie?" or "Do you have a pencil?" This example illustrates a point made above. We could teach "No, I don't" soon after teaching "Do you have a pencil?" In this case, it would probably be taught rather early in the course. If taught in conjunction with "Do you like pie?" it might come much later in the course.

If knowledge of the pattern "No, I don't" is essential to learning the language, provision must be made for its insertion at *some* logical point during the course. It is important that it be built on something the children know. It is important, too, that we make provision for reintroducing it wherever feasible in all subsequent lessons, so that it will become a functional, active item in the children's communication activities. It is *not* important that it be taught within the first, second, or any other level if the other criteria given above are met.

Introducing the Cultural Situations Cultural situations help give meaning and purpose to the learning of the language structures. Some educators prefer to introduce these with a short dialogue built around a given center of interest—shopping, for example—which contains the structures and vocabulary to be practiced that week or month.

Others prefer to start with a folk tale or a familiar fairy tale from which structures and vocabulary for intensive practice will be singled out. One fairy tale, for example, may serve as a vehicle for intensive presentation and practice of language for several months.

Others present the structures and vocabulary through a question-and-answer technique. After several language items have been taught, they are combined into a dialogue, which is memorized or learned to the point of reasonable fluency as a *culminating activity*. When the third stage of reading is begun (see Developing Reading Skills in Chapter 4), structures and vocabulary for systematic practice may also be culled from the reading passage.

Each of these approaches will be studied in greater detail in Chapter 4. Suffice it to say at this point that in any approach linguistic content should be carefully organized, since gradation of structure and vocabulary is essential for efficient learning. Several principles of organization of material are restated or expanded here for your consideration.

Some Principles of Organization

1. The center of interest or cultural topic chosen for study (e.g., recreation in the community) and the structures and vocabulary to be taught intensively should be closely related. Learning is helped by association.

2. Even when the study of structures and/or vocabulary is not based on a dialogue or story, the language items should bear some relationship to each other. If classroom objects are being presented, words about food should not be included. If a new structure is being taught—"May I borrow your _____?" for example—the words used in the initial presentation should be centered around one topic, such as classroom objects, clothing, or whatever group of associated vocabulary items the children know well. Of course, familiar words in any other known center of interest are used in subsequent practice activities.

3. Structures which can be used most frequently in combination with other known structures and which will lead to the development of related structures should be given priority for intensive practice. Consider these two illustrations:

> What's your name?
> What's his name?
> What's your friend's name? etc.

> Do you have a hat?
> Yes, I do.
> What color is it?
> It's red.
> Do you have a red hat too? etc.

4. Structures for presentation should be built on other known structures in the foreign language. Children should be given insight into the succession of bricks or blocks that go into the building of communication. Note this example:

> He wants a cookie.
> He wants a chocolate chip cookie.

He wants a chocolate chip cookie with milk.
Does he want a chocolate chip cookie with milk?
Does he usually want cookies with milk?
Does he want cookies with milk now?

5. Structures which contrast most sharply with English structures should be given intensive emphasis. This is especially necessary with older children. Much more practice spaced over a longer period of time will be needed to overcome sharp conflicts between the native language habits and the new language pattern, e.g.,

Veo a Juan. I see John.
Non lo vedo. I don't see him.
Je suis ici depuis une heure. I have been here for an hour.
Ich muss heraus gehen. I must go out.

6. New structures should always be presented with a very limited, well-known vocabulary. In teaching adjectives of color before a noun, for example, classroom objects or items of clothing would be reviewed first. Then the teacher would introduce the concept of color, retaining the same verb form, the same adjective, and nouns of only one gender in all the examples in the initial presentation. Thus the focus would be only the word order. Later another color could be introduced, but with the same nouns and verb. Note this example:

I have (This is) a crayon.
I have (This is) a red crayon.
I have (This is) a red pencil.
I have (This is) a red notebook.

At least five red objects, all of *one* gender, should be shown before showing blue objects.

I have (This is) a blue crayon.
I have (This is) a blue pencil.
I have (This is) a blue notebook.

7. Only small segments of larger grammatical items should be presented at one time. For example, in introducing personal pronouns, only the forms "I" and "you" might be taught in the early stages. The interrogative might be presented before the negative forms since the "I" and "you" pronouns and the interrogative lend themselves to chain

drills, conversation, and question-and-answer practice—some of the normal forms of communication.

8. A definite sequence of presentation is implicit when the new grammar is based on something that has already been taught, as indicated in paragraph 4. The relationship of the new structure to a known structure was made perfectly clear because each time another element was added to a known base sentence.

Sequence may also be determined by need. An item is presented because it is needed as a normal response in a normal conversational exchange, for example. This does not necessarily mean a prescribed arrangement that cannot be changed. After teaching "Do you have a pencil?" you may prefer to teach "Does he have *his* pencil?" (meaning the boy or girl seated next to the pupil) or "Yes, I do" and "No, I don't." Either sequence is perfectly correct. To illustrate further, in teaching identification, we may teach "Where do you live? I live at _____ _____ Street," followed by "Do you live (near) school?" or "With whom do you live?"

An important criterion in sequence is that what is taught relates back to something familiar—familiar because it exists in the native language or because it has been learned in the new language. Another criterion is that the item is needed in a normal act of communication. Still another is that any item taught should also relate to something to be taught later in the program. Teachers and curriculum writers should be aware of the end result desired so that each item will occupy a logical place in the total program.

By the end of the three- or four-year program, children should have gained a knowledge of all the major structures listed at the beginning of this chapter and others which appear frequently in the reading texts. These should be taught in a logical and psychologically sound arrangement—from the simple to the more complex; from the known to the unknown; from the most frequently used to the less frequently used; from the more generally needed (e.g., "It's a _____" or "How many _____?") to the less generally needed; from the easily demonstrable to the less easily demonstrable; from those which enable children to talk about many centers of interest or experiences to those which are more highly specialized.

9. In harmony with the principle of the spiral approach, the same vocabulary item may be used at succeeding levels of learning, but always in combination with new items of structure which have been

taught. The two following examples can be expanded even further than the illustrations below:

PETS

What's this? It's a (dog).
Is this a (dog)? Yes, it is. No, it's not.
Are these (dogs)?
No, they're not (dogs). They're (kittens).
What does (he) want? A dog.
He wants a (dog).
Do you want a (dog)?
I have a (dog).
I'm playing with a (dog).
I always play with my (dog.)
How many (dogs) do you have?
What color is your (dog)?
When did you get the (dog)?
We bought the (dog) yesterday. (We bought it yesterday.)
Give me this (dog), please.
May I play with the (dog), please?
How much does this (dog) cost?
I'm looking for my (dog).
I can't find my (dog).
I don't have any (dogs).
Don't take his (dog). (Here is) (mine).
Why are you going to the store?
To buy a (dog).
Whose (dog) is that?
It's (his), etc.

FAMILY MEMBERS

This is my (father).
I have a mother, a father, and two (sisters).
What's your (father's) name?
It's _____.[5]

---

[5] Notice that two structures are given. In teaching the *response* to a question, the form "It's _____" would be practiced, since it is the normal response. The statement form, e.g., "My father's name is _____," should also be practiced, since that too is a normal form of conversation.

My (father's) name is _____.
My (father) is forty years old.
What does your (father) do?
He's a (fireman).
(My) (father) is a (fireman).
(My) (father) works every day.
(My) (brother) leaves the house at (eight) o'clock.
What time does your (father) come home?
(My) (father) comes home at (five) o'clock.
(My) (father) likes his work.
What does your (father) have for breakfast?
(My) (father) usually has (coffee) for breakfast.
(My) (father) prefers (pie), etc.

10. Vocabulary should be taught in the context of normal usage—never in lists. Many examples of a word used in a similar *context*—where the meaning remains the same—should be given. Teachers should make conscious efforts to reintroduce words with surrounding words that help establish their meaning as often as possible. An illustration of this technique is given in paragraph 9 above.

When a familiar word is met in a new context ("How *old* are you?" "My book is *old*"), intensive practice should be given in the new context. Both contexts should then be contrasted frequently in functional practice. This is particularly true in teaching older children, who may be starting to analyze the language.

11. Only the patterns used in real conversation should be taught; e.g., children would normally say, "How about a game of ball?" rather than "Would you join me _____?"

12. As we have already stated, only the most functional items of vocabulary and grammar should be taught at this level. In any center of interest or situation, the vocabulary chosen for *active* use should be that which is most frequently used by *speakers* of the language. It should be vocabulary which can be fitted into as many structures as possible. A word such as "thermometer," for example, is not a high-frequency word, since it can be used in only one or perhaps two centers of interest.

The chart at the top of pages 56 and 57 illustrates the integrating of topic and language items by grade or level.

INTEGRATING TOPIC AND LANGUAGE ITEMS BY GRADE OR LEVEL

Topic Identification	Language Items
LEVEL I *	What's your name? My name is _____. My (French) name is _____. My (English) name is _____. What's (his) name? How old (are) (you)? (I'm) _____ years old.
LEVEL II	Where do you live? I live in _____. I live at (22) _____ (Street). What's your (father's) name? How many (brothers) do you have? What does your (father) do? † Who sits (next to) you?
LEVEL III	What date is your birthday? When were you born? Do you have any cousins? What are their names? How old are they? Where do they live? How many (uncles) and (aunts) do you have? Whose sister is your aunt? Whose brother is your uncle _____?
LEVEL IV	Who is (older), you or your (brother)? Who is the oldest in your family? What's your best friend's name? Is your cousin (taller) than you? What does your (grandmother) look like?

* Level I is the beginning level. It may therefore stretch over grades 3 and 4. If language is introduced in grade 1 or in grade 5, for example, adjustments in content will be necessary.

† It is very important not to embarrass children in any way. In talking about occupations of parents, list or show pictures of several types of employment and have the children choose any one they wish. The same consideration should be given to personal items, such as rooms or furniture, about which children may be sensitive.

SUMMARY

In selecting the contents for the language program, preference should be given to situations that are of interest to children everywhere. The language to be used in talking about the situations should be the authentic language of the native speakers. The limited but progressively growing ability of the children to express themselves in a new medium should be given consideration, however.

Cultural topics and language items chosen for inclusion should be intimately related. The same ones may be reintroduced in each grade, but always on a higher level of complexity.

Although vocabulary and structures are selected and ordered with great care to conform to logical and psychological principles of learning and although attention is paid to the sequence in which language items are presented and practiced, sequence should not necessarily be taken to mean a predetermined or unalterable arrangement of presentation.

Situation, frequency of use, demonstrability, simplicity, and contrast with English—each plays a role in establishing the order of presentation of structures. Various sequential arrangements and approaches to introducing the new language or cultural material are possible.

A careful plan will make provision for teaching all the important structures at some logical point in the four-year program. It will provide for continuity and the reintroduction of situation, vocabulary, and grammar at each succeeding level of learning.

It will take into account the language program at the secondary school to which the children will probably be admitted. If the children will enter an advanced level at the secondary school, it is imperative that teachers and administrators at both levels be aware of each other's programs. For example, secondary school personnel should know exactly what the children have learned and what experiences they have had. Elementary school personnel should be cognizant of the expectations of the secondary school with relation to the children's language ability. Only through reciprocal understanding and cooperative planning can a coherent, continuous sequence of learning be achieved.

The curriculum will provide children with insight into similar and dissimilar cultural patterns, through activities and experiences that lead to understanding and appreciation of another way of life.

4

How Are Language Skills Developed?

MULTIPLE APPROACHES

The existing elementary school philosophy and program lend themselves admirably to teaching a foreign language through experiences in which the children participate. They are helped to learn the language by listening to stories, taking roles in dramatic skits, making puppets, playing games, or singing songs—all of which are an integral part of the methodology of the elementary school. They are encouraged to use the new language while participating actively in these or similar experiences. This completely natural and, it is to be hoped, free expression will never be entirely possible again in the more formal, departmentalized secondary school program.

In the elementary school, various approaches are used to develop habits, skills, knowledge, and attitudes in each curriculum area. In music, the teacher may introduce a song by having the children listen to a record several times. He may introduce the use of a new medium into the art class—water color, for example—as preparation for creating the scenery for an assembly program. The language arts class may practice a correct form by writing parents a letter of invitation for the assembly program.

Each approach is different. Each has merit. Each may serve to create interest in the children. Each may have a particular advantage in introducing a knowledge or a skill. Similarly, the use of a variety of approaches in teaching a foreign language is not only possible but also more desirable than the use of any one approach to the exclusion of others.

Although the nature of communication may make engaging in a conversation the optimum outcome of language learning, there are several ways in which this goal can be achieved. Memorization or intensive learning of a dialogue is an excellent way of preparing children to talk together, but it is not the *only* way. Several other excellent techniques are available and effective and should be tried.

The words "approach" and "introduction" underscore the fact that any one of the techniques described below serves two primary purposes: (1) to interest the children in the new learnings because the techniques are pleasurable, and (2) to introduce a new topic or center of interest and language items. Whatever approach is used, the language items selected for emphasis will then be learned and practiced in various language-producing activities.

What are some approaches that have been tried and found effective? How are they used as introductions to intensive language practice? (The techniques discussed here are *not* given in order of preference or degree of demonstrated effectiveness in the classroom.)

The Dialogue When we think of language, we usually think of two people talking together about something that they did, are doing, or are going to do. The dialogue is particularly well suited for practicing authentic language in real communication situations where people listen and react, either by speaking or by performing some action.

A dialogue is an exchange of conversation between two or more people. The exchange may be two lines: "How are you feeling today?" "Much better, thank you." It may consist of five, ten, or even more lines built around a central theme, such as shopping, family, or school.

It is expected that, after they understand its content, the children will memorize the dialogue or learn it well enough to use it without constant prompting, will dramatize it, and will answer questions based on it or adapted from it. As with every other technique outlined here, the dialogue will also serve as the point of departure for intensive language practice of selected items.

Understanding the Dialogue. In order to help the students understand the dialogue or the segment you are teaching that day, you may use any one or a combination of these procedures:

• Tell the story or situation in simple English, pointing to visual materials (if appropriate) as the need arises. These may be real objects or drawings which you have placed on the flannel board, chalkboard, or bulletin board.

- Summarize the story in the foreign language, using the simplest vocabulary and pointing to the visual materials as they are mentioned.
- Teach new words and expressions through association with pictures, real objects, pantomime, or gestures *before* saying the dialogue sentences.
- Give English equivalents sentence by sentence—*not* word for word.

Saying the Dialogue. In order to help the children learn to say the dialogue, or any portion of it, with reasonable fluency, you may wish to follow this procedure:

- Have the children listen to the entire dialogue three or four times. It is preferable to speak it yourself; if this is not possible, use a recording. The first two times, stand at the chalkboard, flannel board, desk, etc., where you have placed the appropriate visual materials so that you can point to them as the dialogue proceeds. You should point to each stick figure or puppet as he "speaks" or "listens." After that, it is desirable to walk to various sections of the room to make sure that every child is listening attentively and can see your mouth and gestures (if you are speaking).
- Say a sentence three or four times and engage in choral and individual repetition, as outlined below.
- Present the next sentence or utterance in the same way. Remember that an utterance may be a word or expression such as "Certainly" or "Of course."
- Divide the class in half. By prompting each sentence, help each group take one role in the two-utterance dialogue.
- Reverse the roles. Repeat this procedure several times.
- Have a more able child stand at his seat or preferably come to front of the room. Let him take one sentence in the dialogue while *you* take the other.
- Reverse the roles.
- Follow this procedure with several children before asking two children to dramatize the lines in the dialogue.

In general, no more than two to four utterances should be learned in any one lesson. (Activities related to the children's own experiences in which you may engage so that the dialogue will assume even greater meaning for them are suggested in the second half of the present chapter.)

In general, three extended dialogues (of more than two lines) should be learned with each cultural unit. One may serve as an approach and contain new items for later intensive study. Another may combine sentences or expressions of the new unit with sentences or expressions taught in a previous unit. This second dialogue is usually called a "recombination dialogue." A third dialogue may serve to illustrate the use of the new language items with another center of interest or cultural topic. For example, "How much does it cost?" may have been introduced with food items. It may be reintroduced and practiced in another dialogue about purchasing classroom items.

In addition to the extended dialogue, any two or three utterances incorporating the new language items and constituting normal interchange should be practiced frequently during the lesson. "Normal interchange" does not necessarily mean a question and an answer. Consider the following examples of increasingly longer exchanges:

    Can your dog do tricks? . . . . . . Yes, of course.
    I like your dog. . . . . Thanks. He can do tricks.
    I like your dog. What's his
        name? . . . . Rover.
    I like your dog. . . . . Thanks. He can do tricks.
                                 Do you want to play with him?
    I like your dog. . . . . Thanks. I got him yesterday.
                                   He can do tricks. Do you want
                                   to see?

The Story or Playlet Well-loved folk and fairy tales to which children can listen many times without apparent loss of interest are used by numerous language specialists as the point of departure for teaching language. Stories selected are usually those in which a concept—and hence language—is repeated throughout.

Familiar children's stories and playlets such as The Three Bears, The Three Little Pigs, The Old Woman and Her Pig, and Red Riding Hood have been found extremely effective as approaches to intensive language practice. Since many of these tales have come down to us from other countries, discussion followed by dramatization can easily bring out and emphasize the international aspects of folk material and the cultural relationship between people from different countries.

Margit McRae has used this approach most effectively and describes in great detail the methodology of what she terms "the whole pattern approach" in her book *Teaching Spanish in the Grades*.[1] (See Sample Materials for a page from this book.)

The story is usually "recalled" in English. Then it is told in its entirety in the foreign language on the day it is introduced. The teacher uses a profusion of pictures, flannel board cutouts, or real objects to which he points at the appropriate time. Some teachers place the picture or cutout on the flannel board or chalkboard ledge as they reach the appropriate point in the story. Others prefer to have all the material visible as they begin to tell the story.

Naturally, the teacher will have to use all the dramatic ability at his command to make the story come alive. The selection of language items to be emphasized depends on what has been taught before and all the other factors considered in planning language lessons.

As will be explained in greater detail later in this chapter, any of the language items in the story may and should lead to the preparation and practice of dialogues, as well as to the performance of other language activities.

Songs Many teachers use songs to introduce new centers of interest and new structures. The French song "Alouette" may be used to introduce parts of the body or future verb forms. "Adios, Mi Chaparrita" may be used to teach possessive adjectives or the familiar form of the imperative in Spanish. It goes without saying that the grammar is not mentioned as the song is being learned, but the teacher will recall sentences containing the grammatical items for emphasis when he starts to teach and practice them systematically.

Since every elementary school curriculum guide outlines procedures for teaching songs, only one or two observations are included here. You may prefer to play a recording of the song several times and then have the children hum the entire song or sing "La-la-la" along with the record. Help them say a line at a time until they know several lines, and then help them sing the words with the music.

Poems may be taught in the same way and may serve the same purpose, but simple, authentic poems are difficult to find. Some teachers like to compose their own. (See Sample Materials for a popular Spanish poem.)

In general, contrived poems or songs are frowned upon because they do not convey the full flavor of the foreign language and culture.

---

[1] Houghton Mifflin Company, Boston, 1960.

(See "Arroz con Leche" and "Blow the Man Down" in Sample Materials.) If they can be used effectively, however, or if you can write lyrics, original music, or poems, by all means use them. Explain that children in the foreign country might not sing the song but ask "Do you think they'd like to hear it?" Any approach which helps teach language as a participating experience is worth trying.

The Action or Gouin Series At the end of the nineteenth century, a French educator, Gouin,[2] devised an approach for teaching language in which the learner speaks as he is performing an action. In teaching a unit on the classroom, the teacher might say (in the foreign language) as he performs each act:

> I'm getting up.
> I'm walking to the blackboard.
> I'm taking a piece of chalk.
> I'm writing my name.

(In some of the common foreign languages, the tense would not be the present progressive, but the simple present.)

Groups of children and then individual children perform the actions and state what they are doing. Questions are asked by the teacher or other pupils: "What are you doing?" and "What's he (she) doing?" The same sentences can be expanded at later levels to include other expressions, e.g.,

> I'm getting up from my seat.
> I'm walking straight ahead to the blackboard.

The actions in the Gouin series should be logical, demonstrable, sequential and should be planned in small "stages." For example, the teacher would not say, "I'm getting up. I'm writing my name." He would give the intermediate steps as shown above.

Situational Learning (Starting with the Structures) As the need arises, the teacher creates situations which will introduce the language structure or vocabulary logically. Let us assume that the teacher wishes to teach parts of the body and expressions concerning illness. He will take advantage of the fact that someone is absent or that the weather is changing and different clothing should be worn, or he can bring in pictures showing a child being examined by a doctor. He will give

---

[2] Francois Gouin, *L'Art D'Enseigner*, 1892.

several sentences about the situation in English. Then he might say, "I wonder how our (French) friends would say that" or "I wonder if this happens in (Spain). Let's find out."

Elementary school children love to set up stores and go shopping. Papier mâché materials or real objects can be used; signs indicating prices can be prepared; toy paper money and coins can be distributed. Children can practice formulas of greetings, expressions of courtesy, and a variety of language items as they alternate in the roles of shopkeeper and "customer." Although "shopping" is often used as a culminating activity, it may also be effective in introducing or approaching the study of needed language items.

Holidays, as they arise, should be the subject of language activity. Holidays in the foreign country will be the subject of plays, songs, and other language learning or cultural appreciation activities. Holidays of the homeland, however, should not be neglected. Comparable holidays in the foreign land—or their absence—should be discussed.

The fact that Thanksgiving is not a holiday in France, Spain, Italy, or Germany should not prevent children in the United States from learning the language items associated with the Thanksgiving holiday, for example. We should not lose sight of the fact that we are teaching a foreign language as another tool of communication. Since American children, for example, normally talk about Halloween and Thanksgiving, we should give them the sentence patterns, formulas, and vocabulary that will enable them to talk about these holidays in the new language.

Incidental Learning Many happenings in the school day can be made to "produce" language. Without special emphasis or formal teaching, routines such as taking attendance, calling for names of absentees, inquiries about the date or the weather, requests to put away materials or get clothing are learned easily as they are repeated each day by the classroom teacher or the children.

If something unusual happens in the classroom or in the school, it can be the jumping-off point for language learning. Naturally, the extent of such incidental learning would depend on several familiar factors: Does the classroom teacher know the language well enough to present the situation—even simply? Is the curriculum flexible enough to allow for the inclusion of additional material?

If a specialist teaches the language and if the happening has aroused interest, the classroom teacher would want to tell the specialist about it so that he could say, "I heard that there was a _____ in the the school. Let's learn to talk about it."

The incident should be used only if the language derived from it would be useful in many other situations. In other words, use the incidental happening as an approach to language learning if it includes high-frequency items or if you can derive such items from it.

Reading Material At later levels of language learning when textbooks are distributed, reading passages, stories, anecdotes, or conversations in the text become sources for intensive language study. Although some of the material will remain a part of the children's passive vocabulary, structures and words which meet the criteria discussed above can be drawn from the text for intensive study.

SUMMARY

The procedures and sources noted here and others are used as approaches by teachers of foreign language. Obviously, any of these procedures can also be used within any approach to reinforce learnings or create interest. There is nothing to prevent the teacher from using any of the approaches mentioned above as an additional activity for practicing language during the development of a unit. Moreover, dialogues, playlets, and songs are excellent as culminating activities in the classroom or assembly.

Today many language teachers and educators favor the dialogue or conversational approach. They consider that the dialogue most closely duplicates normal conversational exchange, which is the very core of language. Indeed, many of the newer textbooks in the field use a dialogue as the introduction to each unit.

There can be no denying that, in the hands of a good teacher, the memorization or intensive study of a dialogue is an excellent approach. But this same statement can be made about the other approaches described here. We would like to recommend *variety* and *flexibility* of approach. Although every unit should contain several dialogues, every unit need not start with a dialogue. If the material lends itself best to a dialogue approach, use this approach, by all means. Formulas of greeting are best introduced in a dialogue, for example. Other language materials may be learned as effectively through a Gouin approach or a song. Some teachers prefer to combine basic sentences into a long dialogue after these have been studied intensively. They find that children often have more enthusiasm for these longer combined sentences or utterances and say them with greater confidence, since all the elements (sounds, structures, words) are familiar.

Whatever approach is used, it is important that two or three formal dialogues, as well as numerous questions and answers and conversational exchanges, be written into every unit of work.

The term "approach" has been used deliberately to indicate that the procedures outlined merely *introduce* a unit of work which may last anywhere from a week to two weeks or even three months. The development of language skills—the end products of our teaching—demands a certain sequence of presentation. It demands, too, the repetition of the language materials in many different activities so that the children can learn to use them freely, without groping consciously for the right word or expression.

What would be a desirable sequence of development? Which activities, appropriate for elementary school children, can help to bring about this natural and habitual control of language?

THE SEQUENCE OF DEVELOPMENT

In consonance with the philosophy which underlies language learning, the language skills—listening, speaking, reading, and writing—are presented and practiced in that order. As you can see, this order is the same as that followed in teaching the English language arts.

The period of time which should elapse between the purely aural-oral phase and the introduction of reading has been a matter of controversy among linguists and language teachers. Some advocate a full year's aural-oral phase; others, a hundred "contact" hours; still others, two months. As with any other educational principle, its application depends upon many variables—the language, the children's age, the grade in which the language was introduced, the children's reading grade in English, the community (Will children see signs or posters in the language?), your ability to maintain interest without books, the children's sophistication, and the children's ability to understand and imitate the spoken language. All these factors should be taken into consideration in determining the length of the purely aural-oral period of learning.

Reading Spanish or Italian is easier than reading French, for example, since there is usually a one-to-one correspondence between sound and letter. Children who have experienced no difficulty in reading English and who may have entered the elementary school well beyond the preprimer stage may require "books" at an earlier level in foreign language learning. An interesting study by Dunkel and Pillet [3] concluded that "in our kind of civilization and educational system some students apparently become 'eye-minded' very early." Other literature in the field is divided. There are two camps of extremists—the "Let's read" and the "Let's not read" advocates and the middle-of-the-roaders. The final decision about the length of the purely aural-oral phase should be yours. Your intimate knowledge of your pupils and your community makes you the best judge of when to introduce reading.

Writing skill is usually developed after reading has been introduced, although in some current experimentation, writing precedes reading. It goes without saying that neither reading nor writing should be introduced, even in a language such as Spanish, until the children have a reasonably firm knowledge of the sounds, rhythm, and intonation of the language, as well as of some of its basic structures. We will return to the subject of reading and writing later in this chapter.

Developing Aural-Oral Abilities

People learn a language by listening to it, by imitating it, and by practicing it. *Listening*—the first stage—must be associated with *meaning*. Although people may be able to hear an intonation pattern or a sequence of sounds and may even be able to imitate it, no real learning will take place unless they relate the sounds to a word, idea, or action which has meaning for them.

Step 1: Establishing Meaning It is important that you clarify the meaning of any new expression or sentence you are going to teach. There are several ways of doing this. You may refer to a song, story, or dialogue which you know the children already understand. Or you may use yourself and the children to teach parts of the body or clothing or colors, for example. Or you may use pictures, objects, toys, gesture, pantomime. In short, you may use any device, object, or action to make sure that the children grasp the meaning of the new language item.

Using more than one picture or object to indicate one concept is desirable. If in teaching the word "pencil," for example, you hold up a yellow pencil and say, "This is a pencil," nothing would prevent the

---

[3] Harold Dunkel and Roger Pillet, *French in the Elementary School: Five Years' Experience*, The University of Chicago Press, Chicago, 1962.

children from thinking you are saying, "This is yellow" or "This is short" or "This is the eraser" (if you are holding it near the eraser). Whereas if you hold up many pencils of various colors, shapes, and sizes, saying each time, "This is a pencil," the correct association will be made.

If absolutely necessary, if the utterance, word, or sentence is not easily demonstrable, or if there is some doubt as to meaning, you may give the equivalent word, expression, or sentence in English; but give the English only *once*.

Let us assume that you want to teach "Good morning." A picture of the sun, a clock indicating seven o'clock, two people meeting on the street, or a mother waking her child may convey the idea that "Good morning" means any one of those things!

Of course, if you are teaching in the morning and greet your class every morning, the children will probably get the meaning eventually, but you cannot really be sure. Instead, you should say "Buenos dias" or "Bonjour" or "Buon giorno" or "Guten Tag" or the expression in whatever language you are teaching in a loud, clear voice once or twice. You will follow this immediately with the English "Good morning" in a softer voice.

Step 2: Modeling the Expression After meaning has been established, you should say the new item five or more times. Stand in front of the class for the first several times, then move around the room, making sure that you can still be seen by everyone.

The language item may be an expression such as "Of course" or "I'd like to," a structure such as "I have a pencil," or a content word. If a vocabulary item is being taught, it should be taught and practiced in a complete sentence, e.g., "This is a book." In introducing vocabulary items, it is always best to give the indefinite article with the noun to indicate that the object is one of a general group.

The number of times you should model the new word or expression depends on several variables.

• Have the children already learned in other language items the sound or sound sequence you are now modeling? If in Spanish they have practiced "Buenas tardes," you may not have to model "Buenas noches" as many times as you did "Buenas tardes." The children already know "buenas."

• Is the word or expression in a new context? If you have taught "Tengo un libro" ("I have a book"), you will have to say "Tengo hambre" ("I'm hungry") or "Tengo diez anos" ("I'm ten years old") many times.

• Is the language item similar to or different from the native language? If there is a difference in form, position, meaning, or use, many repetitions by you will be necessary, particularly if your class includes older children who are beginning to analyze.

Step 3: Ensuring Wide Repetition In this step, children should imitate or repeat what you say while they perform an action or point to a picture or an object. In other words, their repetition should be accompanied wherever possible by an action or gesture which links sound and meaning. For example, the children might point as they say, "It's a dog." They might pantomime as they say, "I'm using my pencil." They might touch their heads as they say, "This is my head." If they are pointing to the door, they should be trained to say, *"That's the door,"* since they are not touching or standing near the object.

The children *in chorus* should repeat what you say. The *entire class* should repeat the new material, because of the support and security which choral repetition gives them. It is important that you give the sentence or expression each time, immediately before you ask them to repeat. It is essential that you train them to keep together.

For the first one or two repetitions, you may say the word or expression in chorus with them, whisper the words, or mouth the words. This gives them confidence and trains them to keep together. In general, it is preferable, once children develop good choral-recitation techniques, *not* to repeat with them; it is easier for you to detect pronunciation problems of individual children if you are not involved in the repetition.

When the entire class has imitated you several times—the number determined by the factors cited above—you should ask groups to imitate you. A group may consist of half the class or a smaller group. You may divide a large class into groups designated by names chosen by the children. You should say the word or expression immediately before you ask a group to imitate you. Groups should also be trained to keep together.

Ask individual children to imitate you only after extensive choral repetition. Giving the model each time is very helpful. The amount of choral repetition necessary before you engage in individual repetition depends on conditions already mentioned, in addition to the children's age. As children enter the adolescent stage, they need more group security before they expose themselves to the possible ridicule of their peers.

If repetition of a complete sentence presents difficulties, you may want to break the sentence into short, logical segments before asking the children to imitate the longer sentence. You may wish to use either of these possible procedures:

1. Break the sentence up from the beginning. In the sentence "He went to the zoo yesterday," the logical breaks are after "went" and "zoo."

    a. Say the entire sentence several times.

    b. Then say "He went," and elicit choral repetition one or two times.

    c. Say "to the zoo" and have it repeated chorally one or two times.

    d. Then practice "He went to the zoo."

    e. Then say "yesterday." Engage in choral repetition.

    f. Give the whole sentence two or three times and elicit first choral, then group, and finally, individual repetition.

2. Break the sentence up from the end. This procedure is usually called the "backward-buildup technique." The segments for practice are the same as when breaking the sentence from the beginning, but you would start with the word "yesterday," then practice "to the zoo," then "to the zoo yesterday," then "He went to the zoo yesterday." Teachers have found that this backward buildup helps them and the children maintain the normal intonation of the sentence.

Step 4: Giving Extensive Practice You will engage in various kinds of practice activities. You may want to think of the division of practice into *drill* (the repetition of the word or expression being taught in a limited, circumscribed situation and with limited vocabulary and structure) and broader practice or *application* (combination of the new material with previously taught material in a normal communication situation).

The steps in both types of practice should be carefully planned and controlled. Practice should start with repetition of new material with no variation or with minimal variation which is carefully controlled by you. If the indefinite article is being taught, you should give practice first in *regular* nouns of *one* gender only. In the foreign language you would say, "Show us a book" ("a notebook," etc.). These are all masculine words in French, Spanish, and Italian. After this practice, you would proceed to practice regular nouns in the *feminine* gender.

After practicing each gender separately, you would engage in practice activities in which children consciously select either the masculine or the feminine form. In a substitution exercise,[4] for example, after having repeated a base sentence such as "Tengo un libro" ("I have a book") several times, you would say "pluma" (requiring "una," then "cuaderno," requiring them to give the complete sentence with "un," etc.). The minimal difference that you would drill and the children would have to select consciously is "un" or "una."

The next phase of practice assumes that the children have sufficient control of the language so that if you ask, "What do you have on your desk?" and you are practicing the classroom objects, a child can say, "I have _____," using either the masculine or the feminine freely, without conscious thought.

Thus the minimal basic steps in practice are repetition based on a model; carefully controlled practice with minimal variation; conscious selection of a language item as a response to oral, audial, or visual cues; unconscious selection or free expression.

A more detailed illustration of these steps based on teaching expressions of age follows. Remember that these practice steps are preceded by appropriate motivation, such as talking about a child's birthday, and by a review of such known items as numbers and verb forms.

a. We help children understand and say, "How old are you?" and "(I'm) _____ years old." They listen to many models and engage in choral and individual repetition.

b. We start a chain drill around the room: one child asks the question of the child next to him; the second child responds and asks the child next to him, and so on.

c. We give a model sentence, "I'm ten years old." Then we give cue words which are to be used to form similar sentences. These may be new numbers or other names or pronouns.

d. We place pictures, some of boys and some of girls, on the chalk ledge or a bulletin board or draw stick figures on the blackboard. A number is written over (or under) each picture. As you or a child

---

[4] Detailed explanations of substitution and other practice exercises are given later.

points, several children are asked to say individually, "He's nine years old" or "She's nine years old."

e. We give children a situation. You might say, "A boy has moved to your street, and you want to find out how old he is. What would you ask?" or "He wants to find out how old you are. What would you say?"

Basic Pattern Practice Activities

General Considerations. Many types of effective drills have been designed to develop in children the habitual control of the patterns of language and to help them attain the ability to talk about many cultural topics in which the same expressions or patterns can be used. Aural-oral (or audio-lingual) pattern practice activities have been given many different names. The names, however, are not important. Nor should the children ever hear them. It is your ability to use the drills when they fit most logically in your presentation that really matters. Not all drills, as you will see, can be used with every language item. The most commonly used aural-oral pattern practice activities are discussed here, with illustrations taken from various topics. (The broader communication activities in which the language habits formed from these practice drills can be used more freely are included in another section.)

In giving pattern practice drills, you will find the use of varied cues or stimuli necessary and desirable. The cues can be audial or visual. To indicate the new word or expression you wish the children to use in a pattern, you may

1. say the word which they are to use in the new sentence
2. point to an object and/or
3. point to a picture
4. show the word on a flash card, on the blackboard, on a flannel board, etc.

The oral cue should precede any other cue since the children will hear the sounds they have to make. They will not be forced to recall the sounds and the word for the concept or object. The oral cue can be followed by object or picture cues. The written cue should be used last and, of course, only after reading is begun.

To strengthen association of sounds, word, and concept, you may hold up the object or point to a picture as you give the oral cue.

Where possible, you should give about six to eight items in a drill before proceeding to another type of drill. It may be necessary to repeat a drill several times until the children can speak with reasonable fluency. A brisk pace—maintained by your immediate prompting if a child cannot supply the new sentence—makes language drill a stimulating activity.

A few other words should be said here about the conduct of drills. With the exception of repetition drills, all drills should be done by individual students. Disorder results when, despite your modeling and extensive class repetition of a base sentence, a cue elicits different responses from the children.

Another point to remember is this: At the beginning level, you should give intensive practice on one type of drill before proceeding to another type. For example, make sure that children respond reasonably well to a substitution-type drill before engaging them in a transformation drill. You may have to restrict yourself to one type of drill for a week or even more until children become accustomed to making the change on the basis of the stimulus you are using, responding individually, etc. Even after a good response to each type of drill is established, usually only one or two drills can be practiced satisfactorily during any one lesson. In initial presentation of new materials, repetition, simple question-and-answer drills (see response drills below), and substitution drills should precede other types. The content of drill exercises should be determined by what has already been taught. Whatever the content, you should give at least two models of the base sentence, the cue, and the response desired. These should be followed by class, group, and individual repetition of the response.

Pattern Practice Drills

1. *Repetition.* Touch the object or picture or dramatize the drill.

TEACHER	CHILDREN
It's a tennis racket.	It's a tennis racket.
It's a baseball.	It's a baseball.
It's a bathing suit.	It's a bathing suit.
xxx	xxx
I'm washing.	I'm washing.

2. *Simple Question-and-Answer.* Touch the object or picture. Notice the gradation from the simple to the more complex in these questions.

TEACHER OR GROUP LEADER   **CHILD**

a. Is this a tennis racket? .... Yes, it's a tennis racket.
   Is this a baseball? .... Yes, it's a baseball.
   xxx   xxx
b. Is this a tennis racket or a baseball? .... It's a tennis racket.
   xxx   xxx
c. What's this? .... It's a tennis racket.
   xxx   xxx
d. Is this a tennis racket? .... No, it's not a tennis racket. It's a _____.
   xxx   xxx
e. Answer with "yes": Do you have a tennis racket? .... Yes, I have a tennis racket.
   xxx   xxx
f. Answer with "no": Do you have a tennis racket? .... No, I don't have a tennis racket.
   xxx   xxx
g. Answer with "no" and add a sentence: Do you have a tennis racket? .... No, I don't have a tennis racket. I have a baseball. (I don't play tennis.)

3. *Substitution.* One word in the sentence is substituted for another word of the same class; i.e., a noun is replaced by a noun, a verb by a verb, an adjective by an adjective, etc. The base sentence given by the teacher is repeated several times by the children. Then the teacher or a group leader gives the *oral* cue to be substituted by one student. Remember that the oral cue should precede the visual cue, since in the oral cue the children are given the word to be inserted in the new sentence and thus not forced to recall sounds and concept at the same time.

TEACHER   **CHILD**

It's a tennis racket (slight pause):
a. Word cue: Baseball. .... It's a baseball.
   xxx   xxx

TEACHER	CHILD
b. Object cue: Teacher or leader touches object.	That's [5] a tennis racket.
xxx	xxx
c. Picture cue: Teacher or leader points.	That's a bathing suit.

4. *Replacement.* A word or expression is replaced in a sentence by another word of a different class; e.g., a noun is replaced by a pronoun. The replacement drill should be carefully graded. This is especially necessary when reading and writing are begun. See the sentences below. Note that the pronoun replaced by the noun occupies the same position in sentence **a**; the pronoun occupies a different place in sentence **b**; the pronoun occupies a different place in the sentence and brings about a change in the verb form (an accent mark, the addition of a letter, etc.) in sentences **c** and **d**.

TEACHER	CHILD
a. Mary has the racket.	She has the racket.
b. He bought the baseball.	He bought it. (It precedes the verb in many foreign languages.)
c. He bought the bathing suits.	He bought them.
d. Give Mary the book.	Give it to her.

5. *Transformation.* Sentences are changed from the affirmative to the negative or the interrogative, from singular to plural, from present to future, etc. Notice the procedure in changing from affirmative to negative and from singular to plural.

TEACHER	CHILD
I have books. I have no books.	I have books. I have no books.
I have pens.	I have no pens.
I have notebooks.	I have no notebooks.
xxx	xxx

[5] Please note that unless the children are actually touching an object, they should be trained to say "that's."

TEACHER	CHILD
He has books.	He has no books.
He has pens.	He has no pens.
xxx	xxx
I have a book.[6]	I have books.
xxx	xxx
I have a book.	I had a book yesterday.

6. *Progressive Replacement or Substitution.* In the substitution and replacement drills the same single element in the slot was changed in each example; in this drill, words in different slots may be changed successively. Children are forced to remember the example which preceded and to make the change the new cue requires.

TEACHER	CHILD
He bought a tennis racket last week.	He bought a tennis racket last week.
.... yesterday.	He bought a tennis racket yesterday.
Mary	Mary bought a tennis racket yesterday.
.... bathing suit	Mary bought a bathing suit yesterday.
.... received	Mary received a bathing suit yesterday.

7. *Expansion.* A word or expression is added to a base sentence in the position where it belongs. You may need to give many examples and repeat the same drill often, since the addition of a word may require other changes in the sentence.[7]

---

[6] Make sure the children understand whether they are to make the entire sentence plural or merely the noun (or pronoun).

[7] In several languages, the addition of "now" changes the verb form.

TEACHER	CHILD
I get up at 8:00.	I always get up at 8:00.
I eat at 8:30.	I always eat at 8:30.
xxx	xxx
He studies (French).	He's studying (French) now.
xxx	xxx
I studied.	I studied them.
I ate.	I ate them.
xxx	xxx
It's pretty.	I think it's pretty.
He's clever.	I think he's clever.
xxx	xxx
It's on the table.	I'm sure it's on the table.
xxx	xxx
It's on the table.	I don't think it's on the table.

8. *Reduction.* A sentence is reduced by changing an expression to a word.

TEACHER	CHILD
I have some pencils.	I have some.
xxx	xxx
Give me a few crayons.	Give me a few.
xxx	xxx
Go to the library.	Go there.
xxx	xxx
Walk to the door.	Walk there.

9. *Integration.* Two short sentences are combined to make a longer, more normal sentence.

TEACHER	CHILD
I have a pencil. It's yellow.	I have a yellow pencil.
My father is tall. He's handsome.	My father is tall and handsome.
xxx	xxx

TEACHER	CHILD
That dog is mine. It's under the table.	That dog under the table is mine.
xxx	xxx
That boy is my brother. He's playing with the dog.	That boy who is playing with the dog is my brother.

10. *Directed Practice.* This is done in three stages.

In stage 1, you or a group leader directs a child to ask a question of another child. You *prompt* his direct question. You direct the child to whom the question is addressed to *answer* the question. You *prompt* his answer, e.g.,

TEACHER	CHILD
X, ask Y "How old are you?"	How old are you?
Y, tell X "I'm eleven years old." Say "I'm eleven years old."	I'm eleven years old.

In stage 2, you or a group leader directs a child to ask a question of another child, using an *indirect question.* You prompt the child who is to answer by whispering *the direct question.* He, of course, asks the direct question in a loud voice. You follow the same procedure in prompting the response, e.g.,

TEACHER	CHILD
X, ask Y how old he is. Say (whispering) "How old are you?"	How old are you?
Y, tell X you're eleven years old. Say (whispering) "I'm eleven years old."	I'm eleven years old.

In stage 3, you give the *indirect* question, but you do not prompt either the direct question or the response unless the children have difficulty.

TEACHER	CHILD
X, ask Y how old he is.	How old are you?
Y, tell X you're eleven years old.	I'm eleven years old.

11. *Translation.* If you wish to make absolutely certain that the children know the equivalent expression in the foreign language, particularly if it contrasts sharply with English, or if you want a change of pace, you may wish—only very occasionally—to engage in translation, i.e., to give the *equivalent* of a *limited* structural item. You and you alone use English. The children then give the foreign language equivalent.

TEACHER	CHILD
I'm hungry.	_____.
She's hungry.	_____.
Mary is hungry.	_____.
The dog is hungry.	_____.
xxx	xxx
It's mine.	_____.
It's his.	_____.

You undoubtedly have noticed the gradation in the drills in the preceding examples. Even after children recognize drill types and can do them with reasonable fluency and accuracy, it is important that only *minimal* changes be required and that they be made gradually. For example, in the translation exercise above, about eight sentences with "it's" (in "It's mine"), "his," etc., would be practiced before you would give sentences beginning with "they're" or "that's" or "The dog is," etc.

In pattern practice drills, it is important to focus on one change at a time; to give enough examples so that children see the general truth that may govern the form, position, meaning, or use of any language item; and to proceed in small steps from the simple to the more complex drills. When a cue necessitates a change in more than one form in *position* and in *meaning*—as would be the case in French in changing a plural object noun to a pronoun—the children will have to arrive at the triple change through the practice of numerous examples focusing on one change at a time.

Developing Reading Skills

Stage 1: Initial Reading When you introduce reading, you should do so with familiar material that the children have practiced audio-lingually numerous times. Use selected lines of dialogues, entire dialogues, stories, action series, fairy tales, etc., that they learned months before, or use the current dialogue. After they develop some reading skill, you may give them practice in reading any appropriate material they learned previously.

You may have the material to be read rexographed, or you may place it on a chart or at the blackboard. Review the dialogue, for example, by having it dramatized. Then read it aloud two or three times while the children follow the written words with their eyes. After this, read each sentence and have the children repeat each one *in chorus* after you. Do this several times. Later, have groups or individual pupils each read a sentence after you.

If the children have not learned a dialogue, you may combine several sentences they know in a logical paragraph or conversation and follow the same procedure. Experience charts in which you record what children say about an activity, such as a trip, a film they have seen, a visitor they have spoken to, are excellent for initiating reading. In any case, *all initial reading should be a written representation of material the children can already understand and say.*

Stage 2: Recombination Reading To develop reading skills such as word recognition or comprehension, make up new sentences, conversations, and stories using only familiar words. Model the sentences and engage in choral and individual reading. Give practice in word recognition by (*a*) using flash cards with words which children will say and then match with a word at the board; (*b*) finding small words in longer words; (*c*) comparing words with English cognate words, if this applies, and (*d*) using all the word-learning techniques—context clues, word families, and root study—normally used in the language arts program.

Comprehension skills can be developed by using the following techniques with familiar material:

    a. "Say the sentence which tells _____."

    b. Say "Give the word which describes the _____."

    c. Ask questions about a sentence which will elicit the words found in the reading. Start with *inverted* questions; e.g., in the sentence "John is a French boy," the inverted question would be "Is John a

French boy?" [8] Give practice with question words the children have learned: "Who is a boy?" "What is John?"

    d. Have the children ask you or other children inverted or question-word questions using "who," "when," "where," "how," "what," "how much," "how many," "how long," "how far." (The word "why" should be used only if the children have been taught the possible responses to it.)

    Stage 3: Reading In the third stage of reading, some of the language items in the reading material will be unfamiliar to the students. The material may consist of what we call "contrived" material. In preparing contrived material, the writer (teacher, school committee, or author) deliberately intersperses some new words and structures among familiar language items.

    Reading material appropriate for this stage may also be found in a language reader which is being used to supplement the basic textbook. Whatever the source, you may wish to use the following intensive reading procedures, which will help to develop children's comprehension of the passage and reinforce their knowledge of structure and vocabulary:

    a. Motivate the reading. Arouse the children's interest or curiosity in the passage to be read by reminding them of a similar experience you know they have had, for example. If the reading is part of a longer story, review the preceding events with them.

    b. State the aim of the reading, e.g., "Let's find out what _____ does."

    c. Clear up any word or concept difficulties. Place the new word on the board. Say it, have the children repeat it, explain it through gestures, pictures, etc. As a last resort, give its English equivalent.

    d. Read the passage aloud sentence by sentence, and ask questions (inverted or question-word) on each sentence to check comprehension. The children's books may be open. With more able groups and after you have given extensive practice in listening to and reading familiar material thoroughly, you may want to have children's books closed. (Vary this—have books sometimes open and sometimes closed.)

    e. Have the children give a summary of the passage, using pictures or words as cues. One child can start, the second can add a sentence, and so on.

[8] In French, teach the "est-ce que" form of the interrogative *before* you teach the inverted form.

f. Extend language learnings using one or more of the techniques you will find in the Activities Resulting in Language Learning section of this chapter.

In the beginning stages of reading, it is generally more desirable to use the technique outlined above. Later, more able groups may read several lines silently and look for answers to questions or other exercises which you either give orally or place on the blackboard (as they are reading). It is important after clearing any vocabulary or conceptual difficulty in the passage:

1. To give the children a definite purpose for reading, e.g., "Where is Joan going?" "What did she say to Rose?" "Complete these sentences: 'Joan is going to the _____.' 'Rose is _____ years old.' "

2. To read aloud the material that you expect the children to read.

3. To time the reading.

4. To reinforce comprehension by doing immediately the exercises you had announced and by engaging in other related activities.

Developing Writing Skills

The fourth language skill to be taught and practiced—but only to a limited extent at the elementary stage—is writing. It is much more important for children to listen and speak than to write at this level. Except for brief—very brief—dictations of familiar material, little writing should be done in class. Any writing should be assigned as homework.

Writing is begun by having children copy familiar material which they can understand, say, and read. A dialogue, a few lines of a story, a chart which tells about an event that they have participated in, or an action series may be the basis of beginning writing activities. Later, children may be asked to write out in full many sentences based on a model. For example, you ask them to "Substitute or use the words in the column for the words in the first sentence and write all the new sentences." Here are two illustrations:

How old is John?
_____ Mary?
_____ the dog?
_____ your sister?
_____ Mr. Smith?

I like to play.
_____ eat.
_____ study.
_____ rest.
_____ get up late.

After sufficient aural-oral training, children may be asked to create several sentences from elements you supply. You may write words such as the following in columns and ask children first to write the sentences across and then to use any combination, e.g., "That man is a student." Make sure the elements you supply can be combined logically. "The dog," for example, would not be appropriate in the first column.

Mr. _____	is a lawyer.
That man	teacher.
My father	policeman.
John	student.

The men	are in the kitchen.
The children	living room.
Mr. & Mrs. _____	house.
The toys	store.

Later—much later, if at all—children may write answers to questions or place words in categories or select the right word, but these activities may begin to take on the characteristics of tests. At the elementary level, the emphasis should be on teaching language skills in a variety of pleasurable activities which will create readiness for the more formal writing instruction and testing of the secondary school.

This is not to say that evaluation or testing should be avoided in the elementary schools. Formal testing is generally not essential, since correct production of language by the children helps the teacher to evaluate progress during each teaching step. We should, however, distinguish sharply between teaching and formal testing. (Evaluation is the subject of Chapter 5.)

GENERAL PROCEDURES AND SUGGESTIONS: SOME COMMENTS

Teaching Pronunciation

• Pronunciation (sounds, intonation, rhythm, stress, pauses) is taught best at the beginning level through intensive listening and speaking. If, however, children make errors in a sound despite many accurate models given by you and/or a tape, record, or television program, you may want to give brief specialized pronunciation practice.

First, make sure the children can identify the sound and *hear* it in five or six familiar words. Let us assume you need to give intensive practice in the õ in French. Say short words (such as "bon," "ton," "son," "mon," "ron," "font") several times. Then help the children *produce* the sound by telling them where to place various vocal organs ("Put the tip of your tongue against your lower teeth; round your lips") or by drawing a quick sketch at the board of the lip position and of the tongue in relation to the teeth. Show by an amusing sketch that the air comes out of the nostrils. As soon as the children pronounce the words reasonably well, reinsert them in complete utterances or sentences and normal expressions and give practice in them.

• Contrasting two sounds, using pictures or words to elicit the sounds, is a desirable and effective technique. We recommend, however, that you teach recognition and production of each sound separately before contrasting them. For example, the French nasal sounds õ ("ton," "son," "ron") and ã ("temps," "sang," "rang") should be contrasted to ensure accurate recognition and production. Teach them separately before drilling them together. To make sure that the children hear and identify sounds:

1. Say a word containing one of the sounds and ask the children to indicate which of the two sounds you are using by raising one or two fingers.

2. Give two words containing the sounds and have the children tell you whether the sounds are the same or different.

3. Give three words and have the children tell you which are the same—words one and two or two and three or one and three.

4. Give four words and have the children tell you which are the same.

To ensure correct identification and production of the sounds, you may (1) give a word containing a sound and have the children give you the opposite word; (2) have the children give you the same word; (3) have a child turn his back to the class, give a word, and have the rest of the class give the same—or the opposite—word.

These pronunciation exercises are best done with minimal pairs,[9] that is, with words which are exactly the same except for the sound

[9] Minimal pairs need not be only the words the children know—although that would be desirable. In using unfamiliar words or word segments, you

you are practicing, e.g., "bain" and "bon," "ding" and "dont," "fin" and "font," "main" and "mon," "nain" and "non," "vin" and "vont." As soon as children pronounce the sounds reasonably well, reinsert them in authentic utterances, sentences, or expressions.

• The normal rhythm of your speech should never be slowed down or distorted in the mistaken notion that the change in speed will aid comprehension. Speak normally at all times.

• If long sentences (anything over seven syllables) have to be divided into segments for easier repetition, make sure the segments are logical. Immediately give practice in the whole sentence again.

• Intonation and rhythm are even more important than individual sounds in giving the language its authentic flavor. Use arm gestures, musical notes, or lines at the board to indicate the rise and fall of your voice.

• If you correct the pronunciation of a word in a pupil's answer, you may give him practice in that word alone, but have him say the entire sentence immediately after.

Presenting Language Items

• Any language form that causes difficulty should be reintroduced and practiced often.

• Exceptions to a form should not be given on the same day—or even in the same week—that the new form is presented.

• Before children learn about an exception, they should be helped to acquire insight into the general features of the language item—particularly if it is different from the native language in distribution as well as in form. For example, in teaching French adjectives of color, you would teach first the ones whose sounds are the same in both masculine and feminine forms. You would not teach the adjective "white" ("blanc"), which changes its form.

• Previously taught language patterns and vocabulary items should be reintroduced as often as possible in combination with new language items.

• When you present and practice a new pattern, use limited known vocabulary. For example, if you are teaching a pattern such as "What do you need?" "I need _____," make use of familiar vocabulary.

---

may explain that they will meet these words or segments soon and that they need to learn to hear and say the sounds.

- When you introduce new vocabulary, use known patterns, e.g., "These are apples," "These are grapes," "I need a pound of apples," and "I need a pound of grapes," etc.
- The items in the early pattern practice exercises should be arranged in definite order (all masculine, all feminine, all singular, or all plural), e.g., "How much is the notebook (the book, the pencil)?" Only one type of language item should be practiced at one time in the pattern practice drills. The more difficult progressive replacement drill should *follow* the simpler drills.
- Language should be practiced with different stimuli and in different normal situations. For example, the sentence above could be practiced by the teacher or a child saying "the notebook," by showing a picture of a notebook, by pointing to a notebook, or by showing the word "notebook." The sentence can be practiced meaningfully in a stationery-store buying situation, in a telephone conversation between two friends, or in a conversation between mother and child.
- Children should be given practice in using polite forms ("Yes, I'll be happy to _____"), in connecting two ideas ("It's a nice notebook, but I don't need a notebook"), and in giving multiple responses to a question or to a statement ("That's a nice doll." "Thank you. I got it yesterday. Do you want to hold it?").
- They should also be given practice in the short forms which are normally used in communication. As a response to the question "What's your name?" the normal form would be "John" or "Mary," for example. If you want to give practice in complete sentences, make the fact very clear by saying, "Let's learn to use the whole sentence now" or by asking questions or giving directions which *normally* elicit a long answer, e.g., "Stand and present yourself." "My name is (John _____)." "What did you do yesterday?" "I went to visit my grandmother."
- Children should be shown how to use the same pattern or expression in a variety of situations; e.g., "I don't know. What time is it now?" can be used as a response to anything from "When will this class be over?" to "Is Daddy coming home soon?"

Developing an Appreciation of the Foreign Culture

- A foreign country corner of the regular classroom should contain real objects, dioramas, posters, and any other materials that reflect the culture of the people whose language the children are learning.

How Are Language Skills Developed?

- The foreign language should be used with gestures and expressions typical of the culture.
- Foreign visitors should be encouraged to speak to the class.
- Persons who have visited the foreign country should also be invited to talk to the class.
- Films, filmstrips, tapes, and records should be introduced to give an authentic picture of the foreign culture. Follow-up activities should be carefully planned.
- Songs and dances of the foreign land should be learned.
- Holidays of the foreign land—whether different from or similar to our own—should be discussed at appropriate times.
- Features of the foreign culture that will interest the children should be brought into the discussion whenever logical; e.g., in discussing breakfast, the teacher would say, "Children in _____ usually eat _____ for breakfast."
- Aspects of geography and history that may have influenced the history of the children's native land—place names perhaps—can be studied.
- Biographies of men who have gained fame in fields of endeavor related to other curriculum areas can be read and then discussed in class.
- Culminating activities in the assembly may be centered about some historical event in the foreign land.
- A trip can be made to a neighborhood, museum, restaurant, or store that reflects some aspect of the foreign culture.
- An imaginary trip to the foreign country, necessitating some discussion of history, geography, or customs (hotels, meals, etc.), can be planned.
- If possible, easy readers used by children in the foreign country should be obtained. These can be displayed and read aloud by you or by the children themselves.
- Any discussion of a feature of a foreign culture should be *preceded* by a discussion of that same feature in the children's experience. They will understand different mealtime hours in Spain, for example, if they first "recall" their own mealtime hours.
- At this stage, children will gain an appreciation of culture as they become increasingly aware that the foreign children talk about all the things they talk about. No systematic presentation of specific

aspects of history, geography, etc., need be undertaken at the beginning level.

• Some features of geography and history will be learned as you use place names ("Santa Barbara," "New Orleans") and words ("rodeo," "opera"), talk about places to which children in the foreign country go for holidays, or plan an imaginary trip to the foreign land.

Activities Resulting in Language Learning Activities in the language class should be selected primarily for the growth they will produce in one of the language skills or in the integrated act of communication. Everything said or done during the language period should foster the use of the authentic forms of language. Puppet making, for example, may be used to give practice in expressions such as "What are you making?" "His eyes and nose." "What do you need?" "A paper bag, scissors, glue." "What will you call (him)?"

You will note that many of the activities below are interrelated—one has to listen in order to hold a conversation—but they will be listed separately under the language abilities to which they make the greatest contribution. Children learn through engaging in the following activities.

AURAL ACTIVITIES

1. Listening to the teacher modeling sentences or utterances, giving directions, asking questions, reading, giving a dictation.
2. Listening to contrasting sounds or intonation patterns in pronunciation-emphasis periods.
3. Listening to visitors.
4. Listening to other children making statements, asking questions, etc.
5. Listening to recordings (discs or tapes) of dialogues, plays, or songs.
6. Listening to a television program, to the radio, to a movie, or to a play.
7. Interviewing someone.
8. Engaging in a conversation.

ORAL ACTIVITIES

1. Repeating words, expressions, or sentences with the class, group, row.
2. Repeating words, expressions, or sentences individually.

3. Responding to directions and telling what they are doing.
4. Formulating directions for other children to follow, e.g., "Walk to the door."
5. Answering questions. The questions, as you know, may be of several types. They should be carefully graded. Children must be told exactly what is expected of them.
    a. A "yes" question—"Answer with 'yes.' Do you have a brother?" "Yes, I do."
    b. A "no" question—"Answer with 'no.' Do you have a dollar?" "No, I don't."
    c. A "no" question with an *added* sentence giving other information—"Answer with 'no' and add another sentence. Do you have a brother?" "No, I don't have a brother. I have a sister."
    d. An inverted question—"Is Red Riding Hood taking food to her grandmother?"
    e. A question-word question ("who," "what," "how," "when," "where," "how much," "how far," "how long," "why," etc.) "Where does her grandmother live?"
    f. A choice question—"Do you like vanilla ice cream or chocolate ice cream?"
    g. A patterned-response question—no matter what question is asked, the children give a carefully controlled response, e.g., "Where's the book?" "Where's your father?" "Who's that man?" "I'm sorry. I don't know." "I'll find out."
    h. Free questions (based, however, on a dialogue, a reading passage, or an activity in which the children are participating or have participated)—"What do you like to do on Sunday?"
6. Formulating questions of the type outlined in paragraph 5 above, which they ask of you or of other children. A very good device is to have individual children ask you a question, the answer to which you have been practicing. This affords you the opportunity of giving the correct model of the answer again. It prevents singling out and embarrassing a child who may have made pronunciation errors in his answer.
7. Engaging in the types of oral practice activities (substitution drills, replacement drills, etc.) indicated in the previous section.
8. Engaging in chain drills. These may be of several types:
    a. Pupil 1 asks pupil 2 a question. Pupil 2 answers. Pupil 3 asks pupil 4 the same question; pupil 4 answers.

b. Pupil 1 asks pupil 2 a question. Pupil 2 answers and asks the same question of pupil 3. Pupil 3 answers and asks the question of pupil 4.
   c. Pupil 1 asks pupil 2 a question, "How old are you?" Pupil 2 answers, "I'm ten years old." Pupil 3 asks pupil 4, "How old is he?" referring to pupil 2. Pupil 4 answers and then asks the original question of pupil 5.
   9. Telling what they see on a picture or chart.
   10. Telling a story with the help of pictures or other clues.
   11. Formulating questions which elicit given responses, e.g., the response is "The baby is fine." The question, "How is the baby?"
   12. Dramatizing a situation (telephoning, buying, visiting, traveling, etc.).
   13. Engaging in short interchanges, e.g., "How are you?" "I'm fine." "Where are you going?" "To the lunchroom."
   14. Playing language games.
   15. Singing songs.
   16. Listening to several sentences about a person. Giving similar information with the help of a picture about another person, e.g., "Mr. Smith is my friend. He's a policeman."
   17. Telling what they were doing, are doing, or plan to do at a given time.
   18. Telling what is missing in a picture.

READING AND/OR WRITING ACTIVITIES

   These should be done *orally* first, as many times as necessary for fluency. Emphasis should always be on aural-oral activities, even *after* reading and writing are begun.
   1. Reading in chorus or individually utterances and sentences which you model.
   2. Copying material from the board or a chart and reading it in chorus or individually.
   3. Completing a sentence when a choice is given, e.g., "He's writing with a _____ (pencil, eraser, ruler)."
   4. Filling blanks when no choice is given, e.g., "He drinks milk from a _____."
   5. Choosing related words in a group or selecting an unrelated word from a group, e.g., "peas," "carrots," "tomatoes," "meat"; "book," "pencil," "glass," "eraser."

6. Completing expressions from one column with related phrases from another column and inserting question marks where necessary, e.g.,

He's	are you?
How	a pencil.
I have	ten years old.
Her name is	name?
What's your dog's	Mary.

7. Engaging in transformation exercises.
8. Answering questions based on a reading passage or other printed material.
9. Writing a short summary of a passage.
10. Taking dictation.
11. Taking an aural-comprehension exercise.
12. Preparing labels or captions.
13. Choosing words that have the same sound from a list, e.g., "my," "pie," "piece."
14. Indicating which of two sentences is true, e.g., "Tuesday follows Monday" or "Tuesday follows Wednesday."
15. Writing a true statement if a given statement is false, e.g., "Wednesday follows Tuesday."
16. Writing letters of invitation to other classes or parents.
17. Preparing menus or writing recipes.
18. Formulating questions beginning with special words, e.g., "Ask a question beginning with 'who.'"
19. Writing sentences describing people in a picture, e.g., "John is taller than Paul."
20. Composing many new logical sentence combinations from two or three columns of words, e.g.,

Mary	studied	yesterday.
John	went to the movies	last week.
Barbara	saw the circus	two days ago.

21. Classifying things (pie, spinach, carrots, cake, etc.) under various categories, e.g., likes and dislikes.

I like	I don't like
pie	spinach
cake	carrots

22. Formulating questions that will produce certain answers, e.g., "I'm fine, thank you."
23. Selecting from among several listed possibilities the response appropriate to a given stimulus, such as "Have a good time." "Thank you." "He's twelve." "I live here."
24. Giving or choosing from several words the opposite of a given word.
25. Giving a synonym of a word.
26. Giving other words in the same family, e.g., "bake" ("bakery," "baker").
27. Underlining the correct caption of a picture when two captions are given.
28. Giving the correct caption for a picture that has been incorrectly captioned.
29. Writing two questions based on a given statement.
30. Writing a statement about a picture.
31. Writing a question about a picture.

RELATED ACTIVITIES

These should all lead to the development of a language skill—listening, speaking, reading, or writing.
1. Finding and labeling pictures.
2. Preparing picture dictionaries.
3. Drawing pictures to illustrate a word or expression, e.g., the stores on our street, the center of town, a one-story house, an apartment house.
4. Preparing bulletin boards with information regarding the weather, daily plan, absentees, etc.
5. Preparing a calendar indicating days, weather, etc.
6. Making and using puppets.
7. Dramatizing any situation, e.g., setting a table, ordering food.
8. Arranging pictures in the correct sequence and telling a story about them.
9. Using holidays (Thanksgiving, Christmas, Halloween, Easter) to dramatize customs (food, songs, dances, related objects).
10. Singing songs or reciting poems.
11. Composing new words to a song.
12. Coloring objects, preparing dioramas or posters.
13. Preparing a hobby show, an exhibit, a quiz program, a play.

14. Using the telephone.
15. Setting up a store—food, stationery, toy, book.
16. Taking a trip to a place of interest—planning it, deciding on a route, choosing buddies, getting permission, making appointments, etc.
17. Drawing a street map showing the route to and from school, for example, and explaining the route to others.
18. Having a spelling bee or any other language competition.
19. Acting out a proverb.
20. Adapting a dialogue or conversation.
21. Playing any of the language games which will be found in the next chapter or any other game you can devise.

SUMMARY

We have indicated that there are several effective approaches in teaching. To maintain interest, the teacher should vary his approach for each new unit. He should also make every effort to use several approaches or procedures as he develops the unit.

Any approach should serve primarily to arouse enthusiasm for a center of interest or cultural topic and to introduce in a meaningful situation some of the language items which will be practiced intensively. Practice activities should concentrate on developing listening and speaking skills. Reading, when it is introduced, should be a recall of language which the children can speak easily because they have heard and spoken it numerous times. In general, writing should not be done in class. Anything read or written should be practiced audio-lingually at first.

The language learning activities are in many respects those used in developing abilities and skills in the English-language-arts program. They differ in one important feature, however. To ensure habitual control of language patterns, the repetitive activities are strictly controlled and patterned by the teacher. This restriction is necessary so that children will learn that only certain words (nouns or adjectives or adverbs) can fit logically into the various slots of the sentence that is being practiced.

It is important that all activities lead to the *production* of language. Do whatever you know the children will enjoy—take trips, dramatize events and stories, sing songs, play games—but make sure that activities emphasize the need for language skills or reinforce them.

All activities should strengthen the children's conviction that they can say anything in French, for example, that they can say in English. Wherever it is possible, experiences and activities should also foster an appreciation of the customs, mores, and artifacts of the other culture.

5

How Can Teaching Be Made Effective?

CREATING A FAVORABLE LEARNING ENVIRONMENT
In the previous chapters, we have examined in detail some procedures generally recommended by teachers and other language specialists for developing language skills. We must not lose sight, however, of the fact that these procedures are evolved in a *classroom setting;* that the *teacher* guides the learning of about thirty *individuals;* that forces or activities within *the school* or *the community* have an impact on the classroom situation; that the use of *special techniques or materials* can make the development of language skills a pleasurable activity to which you and the children look forward with eagerness and enthusiasm.

This chapter, therefore, discusses some tangibles and intangibles that help to bring a touch of art to the well-ordered, scientifically based "steps" which have concerned us until now.

Developing a Cultural Island Language specialists speak of the desirability of creating a "cultural island" in the classroom. This cultural island comes into being in several ways. To some educators it means primarily that the foreign language is to be used at all times or at least for the greater part of the foreign language period. They recommend that if English is used at all, it be used only during the last few minutes of the period. The simple requests needed for presenting and practicing language items should be given in the foreign language at the beginning of the course and used at all times. Children should learn to react automatically to words such as "look," "listen," "repeat," "say," and "answer." The foreign language period should constitute a complete immersion in the foreign language and culture. No one would disagree with that statement.

There are, however, other ways of creating a cultural island in the language classroom. Let us examine some of them.

• A foreign visitor can be invited into the classroom to talk briefly to the children on a topic of interest to them. The children may ask him simple questions which they may (preferably) or may not have prepared in advance. Even if they do not understand everything the visitor says, his "native" gestures and facial expressions will convey the necessary aura of authenticity. If the visitor plays a musical instrument or teaches a simple dance, the children's pleasure will be even more heightened.

• Children should be given their equivalent names in the foreign language. If a child's name has no equivalent, he may select one from a list that you will make available. The new names should be used from the very outset of the course in all activities.

• Recordings of native songs, poems, simple playlets, or dialogues should be played whenever possible. There are very fine recordings on the market which reproduce the sounds of foreign cities and the countryside.

• At least one area of the classroom (if it is the regular classroom) or the entire classroom (if children meet the visiting foreign language specialist in a special room) should reflect various aspects of the foreign culture. Some items (the flag and map, for example) should be permanent parts of the language corner. The corner should be labeled with a foreign language name. Other items can be changed from time to time, just as you would change displays in other centers of activity in your classroom. A colorful chart or bulletin board may contain pictures (in color) of the unit you are teaching currently. A display case may contain dolls dressed in the costumes of the country, coins, other real objects (castanets, musical instruments, sabots, or caps, for example), menus, tickets, etc.

• A table in front of the case may hold books or magazines with pictures of the cities or villages of the foreign land. Dioramas may also lend interest, as do puppets dressed in foreign costumes.

• Other materials—to be used with the foreign language and other curriculum areas—are easily available, e.g., a picture file, number flash cards, a dollhouse, miniature furniture, toy telephones, trucks, cars, etc., a puppet stage, if possible, toy stores (grocery, stationery, fruit, clothing), and the myriad other items which are so effectively used at the elementary school level.

All the materials should be used to reinforce the concept stated before: Children must be given the feeling and the conviction that language is a functional means of communication and not a school exercise. Anything that can be said in English (or their native tongue) can be said as well in the foreign language.

Establishing Pleasant Relationships We have mentioned tangibles—people, books, and things—which help to create a favorable climate for learning. There are other factors or elements which are as important—some would say more important—in developing in children the ability to communicate in a foreign language. Let us commend some of these to your attention briefly:

1. Use the "you" approach in your teaching. Relate the various phases of the lesson to personal experiences of the pupils. Let them tell you about themselves, their parents, relatives, or friends who have taken a trip or had an experience related to your lesson. Use the children's clothing or books or age or height in introducing or practicing new material. Teach the "you" and "I" forms *first* so that they can ask and answer questions about themselves. Start teaching about the classroom and the things in it before fanning out to the school and the community.

2. Use praise generously but judiciously. Find something favorable to say when there has been some growth in a timid child's ability to contribute individually or when there has been an improved performance. Don't say "That's good," however, if the performance is poor. Say something such as "That's much better."

3. Give children a feeling of success. This can be done in several ways:

    a. Provide many models before you ask for repetition.

    b. Engage in *choral* repetition before *individual* repetition. (About the only exception would be when a child gives his name or address. Even then, the first part of the sentence "My name is" is practiced in chorus numerous times.)

    c. Call on volunteers before you call on nonvolunteers.

    d. Call on your more able students before calling on the others. This gives the less able students the opportunity to practice the correct form silently.

e. Plan your procedures so that the possibilities of a child's making an error are reduced. The techniques mentioned above minimize the chance for errors, as does the technique of having the children ask you the question noted earlier under Oral Activities. (You may also use the technique, however, to change the pace of the lesson or to avoid monotony.) After you have given the correct response, you may wish to call again on the child whose poor recitation may have prompted you to ask for the question.

f. Seat a child who needs help near more able students so that he will hear their correct responses.

g. Give children time to think of their responses. Ask a question, pause, then call on a child by name.

h. Prompt a child if he is having trouble in starting his response.

i. Tell children what they are going to be tested on. Do not spring tests.

4. Give children a sense of achievement. This can be accomplished in various ways:

a. Encourage children to ask questions of other children and of you.

b. Encourage them to act as group leaders.

c. Ask children to act as the teacher. Even the less able ones can point to pictures or turn the hands of the clock.

d. Individualize your instruction. Gear your questions or your assignments to your children's abilities.

e. Leave a drill as soon as most of the children say it reasonably well. Go on to something new, to a variation of the drill or to a recombination drill.

f. Combine the separate skills into real communication situations. Have the children come to the front of the room to dramatize a conversation, give them roles in plays, and set up buying, visiting, learning experiences where the separate language items are integrated.

g. Build new language patterns on language they already know. Give them insight into the building blocks that go into the language.

h. Teach all the items in a unit of work, but proceed to a new unit as soon as the majority of students have attained reasonable mastery of the material in the unit. If there are still rough edges, you can always reintroduce the material soon. Do not stay with one unit too long. Give children the feeling that they are moving forward.

i. If you feel that you should not proceed to a new unit, recombine the material into new dialogues or use the material in a game, but keep achieving more fluency or more accurate pronunciation or more uses of familiar material in *new* situations.

5. Provide a socialized setting. If possible, arrange to have pupils sit in a semicircle.

6. Move to various parts of the room, but make sure all the children can see you at all times.

7. Create audience situations. Help the children show off their new abilities to their classmates, other classes, and parents. When you want a child to say something or to show an item, say "Tell us" or "Show us"—never "Tell me" or "Show me."

8. After furnishing the accurate model for a sentence or expression, let the children do most of the talking. Question them and have them direct their questions to each other. Learn with them, if necessary, but remember, they are the language learners.

9. Use the special talents of your children or their parents. Many have musical or artistic skills which can contribute to the pleasure of learning.

10. Maintain a brisk tempo in the classroom. Drills should be accurate but fast; language should not be slowed down; hand signals for change of group or for change of type of participation should be used. It is not necessary to say "The whole class—repeat," for example. An encircling gesture of the arms can mean that. Decide on some signals you can use to elicit repetition or response and practice them several times with your class.

PLANNING FOR LEARNING

Teachers who have had little or no experience or training in teaching a foreign language will find it desirable to plan their work attentively so that every lesson will relate back to something that has been taught and will lead to the use of an item or skill in a broader, more integrated language activity. Every lesson should occupy a logical place in a well-conceived overall plan.

Let us consider two kinds of plans you will have to make: the unit plan and the daily lesson plan. All plans should be detailed enough to keep constantly before you not only the outcomes you hope to achieve but also the drills, activities, and instructional materials that can help you achieve them. The fuller and more specific the plan is, the more helpful it will be.

The Unit Plan "Unit of work" is a name given to a broad cultural topic or center of interest which will contribute to the development of skills, attitudes, habits, and information. In the FLES program, the center of interest may be the rooms in the house, for example. The skills would include listening, speaking, and later, reading and writing. The attitudes would include appreciation of another culture and sustained interest in language study. The habits would include making appropriate changes in forms or placing words in the proper position. The information or knowledge would include aspects of language and culture.

In some language textbooks, the unit may be outlined to some extent. It may contain one or two dialogues, some structural patterns, some vocabulary items, and several drills. It may also contain one or more pictures and suggestions for games or songs.

Where no textbook is used, similar information may often be found in a city or state curriculum guide. Where none of these exists, you will have to plan the large units of work that will later be divided into daily lessons. What are the essential elements that you will have to keep in mind?

Your unit plan should include:

The cultural topic or center of interest

A limited number of language items—structures, formulas, words to be emphasized in teaching

Duration of the unit—two weeks, a month, or more

Major objectives—development of a skill or components of a skill and insights into a facet of culture, for example

Instructional materials—dialogues, stories, pictures, objects, books, flannel board, clock, etc.

Approach—dialogue, fairy tale, action series, etc.

Specific experiences and activities—reviews, drills, games, songs, puppet making, reading, a trip, etc.

Expected outcomes—knowledge of pronunciation; form, position, meaning, and use of a structure; vocabulary words; ability to make structural changes, to respond, to read, to write

Method of evaluation—an oral test, a written test, a play

Sources of information—a bilingual community member, the language specialist, for example

Dividing the Unit After these broad categories are clearly outlined, you will have to plan the division of the items in the unit into logical, sequential, and manageable daily lessons. Let us assume your center of interest is shopping for clothing at the end of the first level, that is, at the end of the fourth grade (assuming that language had been introduced in the third grade). The language items may include —depending, as always, on what has been taught before—such structures as:

> I need a (hat).
> I like this (hat).
> I don't like this (hat).
> This (hat) is (small).
> I want a (brown) (hat).
> I don't want a (brown) (hat).
> This (hat) is (pretty).
> May I have this (hat)?

The vocabulary may include several items of outer clothing and adjectives of color and size.

An Illustration of a Possible Division

First day (approach to the unit)—a story, a dialogue, helping the children recall a shopping experience they have had.

Second day—the names of about five articles of clothing with the indefinite article ("a," "an") used with familiar structures such as "Show us a (coat)." "Point to a (coat)." "Where is a (coat)?" "What's (this)?"

Third day—the verb "need" ("I" and "you" forms [1]) with the vocabulary items taught in the previous lesson.

Fourth day—the negative forms of "need" ("I" and "you" forms).

Fifth day—the verb "want" ("I" and "you" in the affirmative and negative).

Sixth day—the interrogative forms of "need" and "want" ("you" form only; the "I" form is not generally introduced, since it is not a normal form of conversation).

---

[1] Children should be given practice in the familiar and formal forms.

Seventh day—three additional content words (articles of clothing), the definite article of these words and the five words taught previously.

Eighth day—the verb "like" [2] with "I" and "you."

Ninth day—the interrogative of like [2] ("you" form only).

Tenth day—the negative of "like" [2] ("I" and "you").

Eleventh day—two or three adjectives of color following the verb "be." "The (blouse) is (red)." Use only one gender (feminine preferably) in the singular.

Twelfth day—two or three additional adjectives of color after "be." Use the other gender in the singular.

Thirteenth day—the adjective of color preceding the singular noun. "I want a (red) (hat)."

Fourteenth day—the question form "What color is the (hat)?" with the answer "It's (red)."

Fifteenth day—the forms "he" and "she" with the verbs "want," "need."

Sixteenth day—the forms "he" and "she" with the verb "like."

Seventeenth day—the interrogative forms of "he" and "she" with the verbs "want," "need," "like."

Eighteenth day—"May I have (a) (brown) (coat)?"

Nineteenth day—the demonstrative "this," e.g., "May I have this (hat)?" or "(I like) this (coat)."

Twentieth day—the demonstrative "this" in sentences such as "This (coat) is (white)."

Twenty-first day—the adjectives "small" and "large" after the verb "be."

Twenty-second day—the adjectives "pretty" and "nice."

Twenty-third and twenty-fourth days—a culminating activity—setting up a store and dramatizing a shopping scene.

Notes:

1. Fewer lessons may be devoted to the unit if adjectives of color or the structure "May I have _____," for example, have already been taught in another center of interest.

2. Only the "I," "you," "he," and "she" forms are presented. If you wish to extend the unit to include "we," the plural of "you," and "they," many more days will be required.

[2] Since this is a sharply contrasting form in Spanish, Italian, and German, at least one lesson should be devoted to each form.

3. Only singular nouns are used. If you teach the plurals of nouns with the appropriate plural forms of adjectives and demonstratives, you will need to spend many more hours on this unit.
4. In harmony with the spiral-approach principle, it may be more desirable to teach only "I," "you," "he," "she," and the singular forms as indicated above and to return to the Shopping for Clothing Unit at a later time. At that time, in addition to introducing the plural forms, you may teach names of stores and other language items related to cost and sizes.
5. A reminder: Use the new structures with language items from other centers of interest which pupils have already learned, e.g., "May I have this pencil?" or "May I have this apple?"

In the breakdown above, only the new item for presentation has been indicated. Much more goes on in any lesson, however, than the presentation of an item of language.

You may wish to consider the following breakdown of a language period—exact minutes for each activity will not be given, since the length of the period may vary in different schools from fifteen to forty-five minutes. A good balance should be maintained between listening and speaking, between listening and doing, between active participation (dramatization or song) and listening to a tape.

A Recommended Language Period

Warm-up—a review of courtesy formulas, names, or ages; questions about the date, weather, or absentees; a song; a game; the dramatization of some known dialogue; a chain drill on known language items, for example

Presentation—new material or familiar material in combination with other material, e.g., an approach to the unit (song, dialogue, story, etc.), some new sentences of a dialogue, a new language form or pattern, preceded by a related review, reading, a dictation (when reading and writing have been introduced)

Aural-oral pattern practice

Activities—songs, games, picture study, dramatizations

Notes:
1. In general, in a twenty-minute period, about five minutes would be spent on each of the categories above.
2. Before presenting any new language item, it is important to review with the children a *related language item*. For example, in French, before presenting "J'ai besoin de" ("I need"), you

would have reviewed the "I" and "you" forms of "avoir" and "de" followed by "un" and "une."
3. The *related review* may or may not be a part of the warm-up portion of your lesson. In the warm-up, the review or questions can be on any material the children have learned; in the related review, the focus must be on the specific known language item that will be needed in or that contrasts with the *new* language item you are about to present.
4. Before modeling the new structures, three brief steps are recommended:
   a. Motivate the structure by recalling a dialogue sentence or a song or pretending that you have heard something in English or showing a picture or—the whole world of fantasy is open to you.
   b. State the aim of the lesson. "Today we're going to learn to talk about _____." If you can, *elicit* the aim of the lesson from your pupils. "What do you think we're going to talk about today?" (If you have brought in several pictures concerning transportation, the children will know that you plan to talk about traveling or going from one place to another.)
   c. Review related materials. "We're going to need (these words) in order to talk about _____. Let's see if we can remember them."
5. Each step of the lesson should be connected to the step which has preceded by means of transition sentences such as those we have suggested above. Sentences such as "That was very good" or "That's right" or "Now let's use these" or "Listen to them" will sustain motivation throughout the lesson.
6. Variety of procedure is important in order to maintain the interest of the children; e.g., the warm-up should be different each day. Do not start with the weather or the date each time. Include them at some logical point in the warm-up, but vary the point at which you ask for the information.
7. The children's attention span should be considered in planning a balanced lesson.
8. Each lesson should give children practice in developing the different types of skills needed in understanding and speaking a language.

VITALIZING LEARNING

In addition to the procedures already mentioned, numerous devices and techniques are used by foreign language teachers to give life to their teaching. They may use some techniques to associate sound and concept, others to reinforce learning, others to create a cultural environment. Each technique, if well used, will add interest while contributing to learning.

Except for the language laboratory and the large number of language games, the devices and techniques enumerated below are undoubtedly familiar to all teachers. Many are used by elementary school teachers of other curriculum areas. You will see that they can be used by foreign language teachers as well.

Although the teacher's interest and enthusiasm are the basic ingredients in engendering and sustaining interest, the judicious use of materials adds spice and color to the language program.

Language Games Games should be played with three basic criteria in mind: (1) They should lend interest and variety to the lesson; (2) they should increase the children's understanding of the foreign language; (3) they should induce the children to produce the new language.

Variations of the same games can be used to practice nearly any language item. Possible variations for The Curious Owl, Poor Jim, and No, Not I games have been indicated. You will undoubtedly think of many others.

Although people at all age levels enjoy games, you may wish to adapt some for use with younger or older children. For example, in playing Simons Says, younger children can stand while they perform some of the actions in response to "Touch your head," "Touch your neck," etc.). Older children can remain seated as Simon says, "Put your pencil on the desk," "Put your pencil on your seat," "Put your pencil on your notebook," etc.

Games should be played quickly. Explicit directions should be given. The key sentence should be modeled several times. If the game is to be played competitively (to score points), two or three runthroughs should be engaged in before scoring begins. Naturally, the number of run-throughs and the competition (if any) will depend on such factors as age and interest.

A random list of language games with special notes, where relevant, follows:

THE CURIOUS OWL (SIMPLE VERSION)

This is a chain practice game. Child 1 asks child 2 a question. Child 2 answers the question and asks the same question of child 3.

Notes:
1. Establish an *order* for the game (children next to each other or in back of each other).
2. Break the chain in one section of the room after six to eight children have participated. Start the same chain in *another* section. This procedure is especially important when the class is large.

THE CURIOUS OWL (MORE DIFFICULT VERSION)

Child 1 asks child 2 a question, e.g., "How old are you?" Child 2 answers. Child 3 asks child 4, "How old is he (she)?" referring to child 2. Child 4 answers. Child 5 begins the chain again by asking child 6, "How old are you?"

I'M THINKING OF

The teacher and a child or two children as partners stand together at the front of the room. The teacher or a child chooses an item from a group of items the class has been learning. He whispers it to his partner, saying, "I'm thinking of a _____ (number, name, date, month, time, sport, activity, etc.)." He calls on other children in the class to guess what he is thinking of:
Individual: Is it _____ ?
Teacher (or leader): No, it's not _____ .
Teacher (or leader): Yes, it is. It's _____ .

ADD–ON

This is played with pictures, real objects, or verbal clues alone.
Child 1: I see a living room.
Child 2: I see a living room and a kitchen.
Child 3: I see a living room, a kitchen, and a bathroom.
Child 4: I see a living room, etc.
or
Child 1: I like milk.
Child 2: I like milk and pie.
Child 3: I like milk, pie, and cake.

Notes:
1. The game with the verbal clues alone is more difficult, as it forces students to remember the names of items without visual association.
2. You may wish to play the game in categories (food, rooms, games, etc.) or with random items placed on your desk or on a bulletin board.

OH, NO; NOT I

The teacher or a child makes a statement beginning with such words as "I hear that." What the teacher "heard" should be a statement that the child to whom it is made will want to deny. He will say that someone else is responsible. That student will say that someone else is responsible, etc.
Teacher: I understand you came late this morning.
Child 1: Oh, no; not I. I didn't come late. He did.

Notes:
1. Responses can be varied and expanded in many ways, depending upon the knowledge of the children, e.g., "I *always* come early (on time)" or "I'm *never* late to school" or
Teacher: You're very sad, aren't you?
Child 1: No, I'm not sad. I'm very happy, but I think _____ _____ is sad.
2. Use your knowledge of the children to inject humor into the remark without hurting the sensibilities of anyone.

POOR JIM

This is very good for practicing forms of "have," "there is," "there's not," etc. Many versions can be played. It is fun to have two children at the front of the room touching or removing the thing named from the flannel board.
 a. Child 1: Poor Jim, he has a headache.
    Child 2: No, he doesn't have a headache; he has a stomachache.
    Child 3: No, he doesn't have a stomachache; he has a _____.
 b. Child 1: Poor Jim. He doesn't like spinach.
    Child 2: He likes spinach. He doesn't like carrots.
    Child 3: He likes carrots but he doesn't like _____.

c. Child 1: What an unusual (silly, rare) house. It doesn't have a kitchen.
(Child removes kitchen and places it on a nearby table.)
Child 2: Oh, no. It has a kitchen. It doesn't have a bathroom.
(Child returns the kitchen, but quickly removes bathroom.)
d. Child 1: What a silly story (referring to Red Riding Hood). It doesn't have a wolf, etc.

SIMON SAYS

This is good for parts of the body, use of prepositions of place, clothing, etc.

Directives are given by the teacher or a child leader, e.g., "Hands on head," "Pencils in desk," "Hands on shoulders," "Hands behind your back," etc. When the directions are preceded by "Simon says," the children are to carry them out. When "Simon says" does not precede the directions, the children remain motionless.

Notes:
1. This is good as a competitive game.
2. The game should be played briskly. Try to work toward immediate reaction to the command—an indication that there is good aural understanding.

A list of games suitable for number practice follows:

BUZZ

The teacher (or leader) indicates a number. The students omit this number and all its multiples in counting. They say "buzz" in its place, e.g., if three is chosen, "One, two, buzz, four, five, buzz." (The equivalent of "buzz" or a child's name in the foreign language can be used.)

WHICH NUMBER IS MISSING?

The teacher or a student gives a list of numbers, omitting one. He asks, "Which number is missing?"

IT'S MORE

To a list of prices or hours, children add an amount set by the teacher or a group leader.

IT'S LESS

Same as the previous game, except that the children deduct an amount.

WHO HAS NUMBER _____?

Make out number cards with numbers from 1 to 25, from 25 to 100, from 100 to 1,000, and above 1,000, depending on what has been taught. When calling on children to recite, to play games, etc., use the numbers instead of names.

HOW MANY ARE THERE?

Use number cards and pictures of any object, person, or animal. Hold a number card in one hand and a picture in the other. Ask "How many _____ are there?"

HOW MUCH?

Write lists of clothing, foods, or sports items on the board, with prices. Ask, "How much did you pay for the _____?" Engage in chain practice or call on children through the "Who has number _____?" technique.

A number of games are suitable for vocabulary practice. They include games of opposites, synonyms, games using the next letter, and guessing games:

OPPOSITES

Two teams are formed. The first person on team 1 says a word. The first person on team 2 has to say the opposite word. If he cannot, his team loses a point.

THE SAME

The game is the same as the one above, except that a synonym is called for.

THE SECOND LETTER

A child on one team gives a word. The child on the other team has to give a word that begins with the next letter of the alphabet. (Eliminate some letters in advance.)

WHAT IS IT?

A description is given, e.g., "It has four legs. It's made of wood." Children on opposing teams have to say, "It's a chair."

WHO AM I?

A child goes up to the front of the room and turns his back. Another child taps him and whispers something. He has to guess who it is: "Is it _____?" or "Are you _____?" or

A job description is given: "I cut meat." A child has to say "You are a butcher."

TWENTY QUESTIONS

One child is sent out of the room while the others decide on an object, person, or animal. When the child returns, he asks questions such as "Is it in the room?" "Is it big?" "Is it red?"

PANTOMIME

A proverb or a familiar concept of some kind can be acted out by a member of one team. Members of the other team have to guess what the action is. They make statements identifying the action, for example, "The book is difficult." "The boy is tall and handsome." "A stitch in time saves nine."

WHAT DOESN'T BELONG?

Members of one team give four words orally, one of which does *not* belong in the list—"milk," "bread," "hat," "pear." Before the count of three the other side has to tell which word does not belong.

WHAT'S MISSING?

A child is sent out of the room. Something is removed from a table in his absence. He has to guess what is missing.

ACTION SERIES (SOMETIMES CALLED THE GOUIN SERIES)

A child is called upon to perform an action in the classroom at some distance from his seat. The teacher or another child makes a request, e.g., "Go to the door and open it." In a more difficult version, the child has to say what he is doing each step of the way, e.g., "I'm getting up. I'm walking to the side of the room. I'm passing the teacher's desk," etc. The game may be made to produce even more language if questions are asked by the teacher or by other children as the first child is performing the action, e.g., "What is he (she) doing?" "What did he do? What has he just done?" Questions may also be directed to the first child, e.g., "What did you do?"

IT'S NOT (ANOTHER VERSION OF I'M THINKING OF OR TWENTY QUESTIONS)

The game consists of a person (teacher or leader) who knows the answer telling the class three things the object or person is not, e.g., "He's not a butcher. He's not a tailor. He's not a mechanic." The class then proceeds to make other guesses.

LOTTO (GOOD FOR NUMBERS AND LETTERS)

Each child prepares a card with columns about an inch apart labeled "A," "E," "I," "O," "U." He divides the card into six rows. In column A, he writes any number from one to ten; in column E, any number from ten to twenty; in column I, any number from twenty to thirty; in column O, from thirty to forty; in column U, from forty to fifty. He keeps about fifty bits of blank paper or cards in an envelope.

The teacher has oaktag cards marked with letters and numbers. He (or a child) scrambles the letters in a box and then picks a card and calls the number. Children at seats are to cover the numbers called. The first child who wins (according to rules set by the teacher, e.g., the top line across or the whole card) cries, "Lotto!"

SHOW AND TELL

The teacher or group leader gives each child a picture within one or several centers of interest. Then he asks questions or gives directions such as: "Who has the _____?" The pupil who has the picture answers, "I have the _____."
Teacher (or group leader): Show us the _____.
Pupil: Here is the _____.

Teacher (or group leader): What color (shape) is the _____? What do you have, _____? (naming a child) What does he (she) have? etc.

Many other games are possible. You should add to your repertoire at every opportunity.

Pictures A picture file should be an integral part of every language classroom. The preparation of the file may be a cooperative activity of teacher and children. The very selection and mounting of the pictures can help children acquire language. Sentence patterns in the foreign language such as "Can you find _____?" "Can you bring in _____?" and "Let's look for _____" can be practiced naturally.

A file of pictures of both individual objects and situations (people eating, playing, talking, etc.) is invaluable in (1) motivating learning, (2) overcoming limitations of children's personal experience, (3) clarifying words and concepts, (4) reducing learning time by associating sound and concept without lengthy explanation, (5) making varied practice possible.

Some basic criteria in preparing pictures include:

• Pictures should have no captions—when reading is begun, related flash cards can be prepared to permit matching drills.

• Pictures for class use should be large enough to be seen by the entire class.

• They should be uncluttered.

• They should be in color wherever possible so that language related to colors can be practiced when colors are presented, e.g., "What color is the _____?" "How many red _____ are there?" "Who is wearing the blue _____?"

• There should be more than one picture of an object not only to avoid the confusion mentioned previously but to enable you to practice plurals.

In addition to large pictures (about 12 by 14 inches), smaller cut-out pictures for use with the flannel board or vocabulary wheel (explained below) are valuable. Children will also want to have sets of smaller pictures for making picture dictionaries or illustrating centers of interest in their notebooks.

Many teachers prefer to mount several pictures related to a center of interest on one large piece of oaktag. The large chart enables them to conduct some drills or games more briskly than would be possible if they had to uncover individual pictures, e.g., "I see a pencil (a pen, a ruler)" or "I don't want a pencil. I want a ruler." (In this case, the teacher or group leader points to one object and then quickly to another.)

Some Uses. Before giving a suggested list of pictures, let us indicate one or two effective uses for them. There are many, many more, since picture cues can be used with any oral practice activity.

In presenting a new word, show two or more pictures of the same concept and say the word in a complete sentence many times, e.g., "This is a cat" or "It's a cat." Children (class, groups, individuals) point and say, "That's a cat" or "It's a cat." Give directions such as "Show us" or "Give (me)." Formulate or have children formulate questions such as "Where is the _____?" and "What's this?"

In engaging in various practice activities, in a substitution exercise, say the base sentence "I need a pen." Point to other individual pictures of objects. Children substitute the new word for the word "pen." In a replacement exercise, assume that "I need a pen" is the base sentence. Point to pictures of children or adults. The children say, "The boy needs a pen," "John (if names have been given to pictures) needs a pen," or "The girls need a pen," "Mary needs a pen," "She needs a pen."

In teaching more extended structures, combine pictures of people and various means of transportation. Stack sets of pictures and uncover them to make sentences such as "The boy took a bus" and "The women went by train." Combine pictures of people, vehicles, and places to practice sentences such as "How is the boy going to school?" "By bus (train, taxi)," "The man is going to the library by car," "The children went to the zoo by taxi."

The use of pictures for testing will be discussed below.

A Recommended List. The following pictures should be included in the class file:

CITY LIVING

School

Personnel—principal, nurse, custodian, librarian
Rooms—gymnasium, auditorium, cafeteria, shops, nurse's office, principal's office, classrooms
Instructional materials—bulletin boards, books, pencils, charts, etc.

Home

Rooms—bedrooms, bathroom, kitchen, living room, dining room
Furniture—dresser, closet, tables, chairs, lamps, rugs, stoves, refrigerators, iceboxes, bookcases, beds (mattresses, sheets, blankets), pillows
Utensils and tools—knives, forks, spoons, plates, saucers, cups, broiler, pots, pans, hammer, scissors
Home activities—cooking, eating, sweeping, washing, sewing, dressing, reading, studying, caring for health and appearance (brushing teeth, combing hair, etc.)
Meals—setting the table, serving, types of food for breakfast, lunch, dinner, snacks, parties
Recreation—radio, television, cards, word games, checkers, parties, books, phonograph, crossword puzzles, knitting, sewing, cooking, others in your community
Holidays—Symbols used (jack-o'-lantern, Christmas tree, turkey)

Community

Post office—various departments—stamps, air mail, envelopes, parcel post, inquiry window, money orders, forms (parcel post), mailboxes
Police—uniforms, equipment, different types of police jobs, traffic
Fire—fire house, equipment, uniforms, people performing various duties
Business establishments—stores (grocery, meat shop, candy store, vegetable market, beauty parlor, pet shops, chain stores, drugstores, others)
Sanitation—street cleaners, trucks
Health—doctors, nurses, ambulances, clinics, hospitals
Occupations—factories, mechanics, sales clerks, manual jobs, armed services, professional
Places of worship
Transportation—
    Signs such as—stop, go, right, left, uptown, downtown, one-way, detour, this way out, exit, entrance, etc.
    Types of transportation in the neighborhood—bus, train, car, bicycle, scooter, wagon, carriage, truck
Recreation

In the neighborhood—playgrounds, schoolroom, gym, sports equipment (such as gloves, bat, ball)
Out of the neighborhood—skating rinks, movies, library, museums, beaches, ball parks, zoo, organizational activities such as Boy Scouts
Weather—rain, sun, clouds, snow, snowman
Seasons
Holidays

The foreign country

Holidays—religious, political, national, etc.
Places of interest
Homes, houses, stores, foods, customs

COUNTRY LIVING

Farms

Houses
Buildings
Barn
Silo
Chicken houses
Fields
Crops
Orchards
Pastures
Brooks
Woods
Farm equipment—tractors, trucks, hoe, spade, fork
Animals—domesticated: cows, horses, pigs, sheep, chickens, ducks, geese, dogs, cats; wild: deer, rabbit, squirrels, bears
Fish and wild birds

Rural community life

Recreational—country dances, hay rides, skating, sleighing, swimming, horseback riding, country fairs, carnivals, picnics
Places of worship
Schools, library

Homes

Interiors
    Farm kitchen and utensils
    Bunks
    Living room

Transportation

School bus, automobiles, station wagon, trains, bus

Communication

Mailman, mailboxes, letters, mail-order catalogues, magazines, newspapers, telephone

Materials or Props Several terms are used in discussing the real, miniature, or toy objects which the foreign language teacher finds valuable in setting up the real situations about which the children will communicate. From the world of the theater and television, we have borrowed the word "props." It is fast replacing the more familiar "realia."

Props and pictures may be used in similar ways. Pictures may be easier to handle, and in some cases are more effective than props. In teaching size, a picture of an elephant next to a dog could show relative size, whereas a toy elephant and a toy dog would not. On the other hand, props or miniature toys would be invaluable in creating a farm scene.

Material should be chosen carefully and used judiciously. If you are giving practice activities in a substitution drill—"I see a cow," "I see a dog," for example—you can create interest and provide variety by using pictures one day and toy animals the next. To indicate action or movement, props are often preferable to still pictures. If you need to hide things or to pull things out of a basket in a game, the props are also superior to pictures.

A list of general props is given here. The need for special props is determined by the language you are teaching. Some props may be real; some may be made of papier mâché or cardboard; some may be toys or miniatures (furniture for the dollhouse, for example). Please remember that these are good to have to supplement *your* gestures or dramatizations or your pictures. You can teach an excellent lesson without expensive toys. As a matter of fact, simple props that are made by you and the children are often the most effective.

Useful Props
Clock with movable hands
Large cardboard maps of North America, of the foreign country, and the world
Globe
Puppets (at least two, a boy and a girl)
Birthday cake (cardboard) and candles
Street lamp (streets and avenues)
Flannel board (to be explained below)
Classroom objects (pencils, crayons, books, and rulers of various colors and sizes)
Calendars—of the week, the month, the year
Pocket chart (to be explained below)
Sports equipment (baseball, football, etc.)
Animals (dog, cow, horse, etc.)
Table-setting equipment (silver, dishes)
Dollhouse
Miniature furniture
Menus
Tickets
Christmas cards
Doll and doll clothing
Vehicles (trains, buses, etc.)
Toy telephones
Puppet stage
Boxes, bags, etc.

The Flannel Board or Flannelograph This useful teaching adjunct during any step in the teaching process can be purchased, or you may construct one easily—and inexpensively—by tacking a square of coarse white or green flannel (the cheaper, the better) to a 24- by 24-inch piece of cardboard, oaktag, or wood. Pictures or cutouts to which a small piece of flannel or sandpaper (rough side out) has been glued may be placed on it. Cutouts of different colored flannel cloth are also effective, since they adhere to the board with no pressure. The cutouts can be moved easily from one position to any other.

Some Suggested Uses

1. Let us assume that your cultural topic or center of interest is the furniture in a room. You may want to place the items on the flannel board as you teach the name of each one. In chorus and then indi-

vidually, children say, "That's a couch" or whatever the item is as they point to it.

Practice activities with vocabulary items may include the following: One child at his seat says to another, who is standing at the flannel board, "Show (us) the couch" or "Where is the couch?"

A child says to another child or the teacher, "Please point to the lamp."

A child asks, "Is this a lamp or a chair?" The answer may be "It's a _____" or "It's not a _____. It's a _____."

A child asks, "What's this?" The response may be "It's a _____."

The cutouts may then be removed from the board and placed on a desk. The teacher or the child may say, "Find the couch (lamp, TV set, etc.), and place it on the board. Place the table in front of the couch. Place the couch in front of the window. Place the lamp to the left of the door," etc.

Children may then be asked to show how the furniture is arranged in their homes, e.g., "The lamp is next to the couch," "The table is in front of the window," etc.

2. Many of the games outlined can be played with flannel board cutouts, e.g., Add-on, Poor Jim, etc.

3. Fairy tales are told very effectively when flannel board cutouts are used. You may place each item on the board as you mention the name: "Once upon a time, there was a girl named Cinderella." Or you may have the cutouts on the flannel board ahead of time and point to people or things as you mention them.

4. Several stick figures (children or adults) made of flannel are an excellent means of indicating role changes in dialogues.

5. A single large cutout of a person can be made a source of pleasurable activity for the children. A figure about 18 inches high is cut out of flannel. Each part of the figure is a separate piece of flannel (ears, hair, head, nose, mouth, neck, arms, etc.). Articles of clothing, such as a jacket, trousers, and shoes, are also cut out. The pupils name the figure and then play with it. They love putting it together, playing Poor Jim with it, dressing it, and talking about its illnesses. (One child would point to a part of the body, and another would say, "He has a headache" or "He has a sore throat," etc.)

As with every other device, the uses of the flannel board are limitless, but it is effective only if it leads to natural—and enjoyable—oral production.

Creative Play Activities Any form of dramatic play may be effective in motivating learning and in simulating situations in which language can be practiced realistically. The activities will differ for various age groups. With younger children, block building, housekeeping, and making puppets and many others can lead to language development. For example, in making puppets, the teacher may ask questions such as the following: "What do we call this?" (pointing to paper, scissors, glue, etc.) "What's this?" or "What are these?" (pointing to his head, nose, eyes, etc.)

With older children, telephoning friends, setting up stores, dramatizing visits, dialogues, and taking roles in plays can offer opportunities for language practice. A buying activity can be used many times, always with longer or more complex patterns. For example, children may set up a school supply store.

Two Illustrations of Conversations. At level I, the dialogue may be as follows:

> Good morning.
> May I have a notebook?
> Yes, here's a notebook.
> Thank you.
> Good-by.

At level II, the dialogue may include the above *and:*

> How much is this notebook?
> It's _____ cents.

At level III, the dialogue may include all the above *and:*

> Do you have a better (cheaper, larger) notebook?
> Yes, I do. (No, I don't.)

At level IV, the dialogue may include all the above *and:*

> I don't want this notebook. I want a notebook with lines. I have one without lines.
> and/or
> I'm sorry. I don't have any other one.
> and/or
> May I have the green one and the red one?

The same type of expanded dialogue can also be used in telephone conversations.

> **Level I:** Hello. Is this John?
> Yes. How are you?
> I'm fine.
> **Level II:** Add—
> May I speak to John, please.
> Yes. Who's calling?
> This is Peter.
> **Level III:** Add—
> Hi, John. Can you come to my house?
> I'll ask my mother.
> **Level IV:** You may add—
> At what time?
> I can come but I must be back at six o'clock. We have dinner at six.

It is easy to see that the possibilities are numerous. The more able children may even compose telephone dialogues from language patterns they have learned or adapt dialogues you have given them. Every topic listed in Chapter 3 may lead to a telephone conversation.

Dramatizations need not be as formal as those outlined here. Any utterances that lend themselves to two children coming to the front of the room and "performing" should be exploited. Many pairs of children should act out the same conversation in one class period.

Puppets. The puppet stage is also a wonderful vehicle for language practice. It need not be at all elaborate—a crate which the children have painted or covered during art period will make a suitable stage.

Conversations may be had with or about the puppets. Puppets are invaluable when, for example, there are only girls in the classroom and it is necessary to talk about boys, their age, clothing, etc.

In teaching a dialogue, you may prefer to use hand puppets. It is easy to hold a puppet in each hand and let each one nod his head when he is the speaker. In the initial stage of presentation, you will take both roles. Later, you will take one and a child will take another. You may then either reverse the roles or have still another child come to the front of the room to take the second role. Then, of course, will come the eagerly awaited moment when two children will manipulate the puppets and engage in the conversation with little or no prompting from you.

Puppets are also excellent for providing the anonymity that some of the more timid older children may need. Their reluctance to stand and recite individually is often quickly overcome when they are hidden behind the stage. Your reassurance that they said the lines very well will usually help them venture to recite openly in class soon after.

Songs Although some teaching techniques may provoke controversies, all educators agree on one: At least one song should be sung during each language period. Songs may be used to introduce a new center of interest, to practice language items, or merely to give pleasure in a shared activity.

Procedures for teaching songs are those used in teaching English songs, except that we give the meaning of the song and explain (by pictures, gestures, etc.) any new words. The explanations, however, may be given after the children have heard the music and words of the song several times.

Although teaching songs has been briefly mentioned previously, you may find it helpful to examine this suggested procedure:

Have the children hear the song two or three times, depending upon its length and the complexity of the melody.

Have the children hum the melody or sing "la-la-la" with the music.

Say the words of the first line.

Have the children repeat the words once or twice in chorus.

Sing the first line with the words.

Have the children sing the first line. Sing along with them.

Teach the second line as above.

Sing the first and second lines with the children.

Continue in this way.

If you have any really serious reservations about your singing ability, play the recording during the steps when you are not teaching the words of the song. You should realize, however, that children are usually not critical of teachers' voices. They are so occupied with listening to the new melody and words that your less-than-operatic voice goes unnoticed.

Your children will undoubtedly enjoy teaching the song to others in assembly or music period. They can also sing at a play or festival to which other classes and community members can be invited.

The Language Laboratory When the use of language laboratories and individual tape recorders began, many people felt that they had no place in the elementary school foreign language program. Current experimentation and reports indicate that the language laboratory, if properly used, can be effective in the elementary school. Our purposes in using the language laboratory are the same as our purposes in using any other technique or device: to develop listening and speaking ability, to change the pace of the lesson, to reinforce learning, to motivate, to stimulate, to simulate reality, and to breathe more life into our lessons.

When one tape recorder is available in the classroom, there are other cogent reasons for using it wherever possible. A few are mentioned here:

• Fairy tales, dialogues, anecdotes, etc., can be recorded by the teacher or by a native speaker. These can be used as an aid in memorization or as a supplementary listening activity after the initial presentation of the material by the classroom teacher. They can be heard weeks after the initial presentation either during the opening warm-up or toward the end of the language period—to change the pace after a formal drill exercise, for example.

• Children are enabled to hear voices other than that of the teacher.

• Children who have been absent can listen to a fairy tale or dialogue they missed.

• Special radio or television programs can be taped for future class or group activities.

• Groups of children can practice language patterns and/or dialogues—practice they may need—while the teacher is engaging another group in a different activity. A jack with six to ten sets of earphones can be plugged into the recorder so that children are not distracted.

• Since the tape recorder never gets tired and never changes its intonation (although it may occasionally run into mechanical difficulty), extensive pattern practice, so important for fluency and habitual control of language, is possible without fatigue or boredom on the part of the teacher. Incidentally, although children do have a shorter attention span than adults, they never seem bored by repetition.

• Classroom teachers who need to develop more fluency can learn the language along with the children.

- Recordings from or about the foreign country—recordings in which both street noises and dialogues are included—create an atmosphere of authenticity and increase the effectiveness of the cultural island.
- When writing begins, children may take short dictations from the recorder.
- You or a native speaker can prepare simple sentences within the children's understanding to accompany each frame of a filmstrip. The association of the audio, the lingual, and the visual enhances learning.
- Recombined stories or dialogues may be recorded and played without extensive presentation by the teacher. Questions to check comprehension may also be recorded or asked by the teacher. Answers, too, can be recorded, with appropriate pauses for repetition by students.
- Children may be helped to develop auditory acuity by repeating model sentences during pauses provided on the tape. These may then be played back so that the children can compare their pronunciation with that of the model.
- Progress may be evaluated by means of the recorder. An effective procedure is to ask children individually to record several lines of a dialogue or story when it is first learned. Each child gives his name and then speaks the lines. A space is left on the tape. Then another child records. A stop watch or timing device (the counter on newer recorders) or a tiny piece of red tape is needed to indicate change of speaker. The space left for each child is long enough for him to record the same lines, plus another twenty or thirty seconds for "priming." At some time later in the year, each child is asked to record the same material again in the space next to his first recording. When the recordings are played back, children, parents, and administrators can judge the progress which has been made in fluency and accuracy.

Many excellent books have been written on the use of the tape recorder. It is not our intention to duplicate what has been said. We would recommend that the recorder be used primarily for listening to songs, stories, dialogues, etc., and for group or individual oral practice of language patterns in the elementary school. In general, new material should not be presented. Not only is it difficult for thirty children to hear sounds and intonation when only one tape recorder is used, but the mouth movements and gestures which facilitate understanding cannot, of course, be seen.

Numerous techniques are advocated for giving pattern practice with the tape recorder. You may wish to consider the following for repetitive practice: The teacher or native speaker says a sentence, the children repeat it, the teacher says the same sentence again, the children repeat it again. In a pattern practice exercise, the children hear the model sentence and the cue, then they respond; they hear the correct response and say the correct response.

To give practice in answering questions, the procedure is similar. (We do not recommend that children practice free answers, except in a language laboratory where they cannot hear each other, since incorrect answers may cause confusion.) The teacher asks a question. The pupils answer. The teacher gives the correct answer. The children repeat the correct answer.

It goes without saying that material—particularly pattern practice material—that is prepared for use on tape should conform to the criteria advocated throughout this book. Model examples should always be given before the children are asked to participate. In general, the material should be within one center of interest; simple material should precede more difficult material; at least five examples of one drill type should be given. Eight would be preferable.

One point should be stressed: Unless you feel really insecure about your knowledge of the foreign language, you should first present what the children will hear on the tape recorder. By far the most desirable plan is to have you take time to listen to the material several times before coming into the classroom so that you can teach the dialogue, story, or whatever it may be. The tape recorder should reinforce what you have taught. It should not do the initial teaching. The exception, as we noted before, may be in teaching a song.

Many other ways of utilizing tape recorders will occur to you as you think of the uses you and your colleagues make of them in other areas of the elementary school teaching program.

Television, Radio, and Movies Many communities use television programs to overcome the shortage of qualified language teachers. Others use kinescopes (filmed television lessons) for the same purpose. As with every other tool, television is effective only when it is used judiciously. The children have to be prepared for the television lesson just as they have to be prepared for films, filmstrips, etc. A brief explanation—in English or, if possible, in the foreign language—should be made in advance to prepare them for what they are going to see and hear. If pencils, books, or notebooks are needed, they should be readily available.

Most important, however, are the reinforcement and follow-up activities. Research projects and television teaching experiences have demonstrated that the classroom teacher or language teacher must listen with the children and reinforce the program content with related language activities as soon as possible after the televised program.

School systems and commercial firms which make use of language teaching television programs usually distribute manuals for the teacher's use. In general, however, these give only brief indications of possible follow-up activities. Teachers will find it desirable to supplement the activities suggested in these booklets with others from Chapter 4. In cases where television is used only occasionally and not as the basic teaching program, the procedures used in showing filmstrips are appropriate.

Radio and sound movies present problems in teaching language simply because the language content is generally uncontrolled. Whether or not you use them will depend on the level of language learning your children have achieved and the nature of the program. For example, radio may provide good opportunity for listening to or learning songs. With respect to films, you may wish to show a film of a scene in the foreign country, eliminating the sound track, however. You or you and the children could later prepare several sentences in the foreign language about the film at the children's language level.

Filmstrips are generally better suited to the early levels of language learning since you and the children can devise captions, using language items that are within the children's ability. Taping such captions, as we have recommended, is very desirable. You can also pause for as long as you wish at each frame and turn back to or skip frames as you desire. The same filmstrip can be used again and again during the course to provide practice on captions, utterances, or sentences at a progressively higher level.

The Utilization of Community Resources In addition to trips that may be taken in the community, the people and places in it may be utilized in numerous ways. The possibilities for developing language skills through trip experiences are endless. When trips are made to places which will clarify or reinforce some concepts about the people whose language the children are learning, they assume even greater significance.

Restaurants, museums, exhibits, homes, or ships—if you work in a community where these are accessible—are some of the places to visit. Visits should be made to "produce" language. Depending on their language level the children can (1) prepare a budget for carfare or meals, (2) set times for departure and arrival, (3) select the route to be taken, (4) plan questions to be asked of the persons at the places visited, (5) talk about safety precautions, (6) write letters to the principal and their parents asking for consent to take the trip, (7) write letters to the place to be visited to ask for necessary information, (8) prepare sentences or paragraphs about their experience, (9) prepare a booklet with pictures and captions which will give the highlights of the visit.

In general, any preparation for or follow-up of a trip taken as part of another curriculum area could be discussed in the language period. The language, of course, would be more limited, and only high-frequency items would be used and learned, but such discussion is an excellent technique for correlation.

The community may be utilized in other ways, too. We can give only general indications, since the population and nature of your community will determine the activities in which you can solicit cooperation.

• A member of the community may be invited to play an instrument, teach a dance, or show slides of the foreign country. Planning and language will include the invitation to the person, the questions to be asked, the refreshments (if any) to be served, the letter of thanks. Follow-up activities ("Can we teach this dance in another class?" or "Can we use this in our assembly program?") should also be discussed.

• A member of the community may be invited to give a short talk in the foreign language on a topic which may be of interest to the children because they are learning about it in another class—science or social studies, for example. You may want to write to the speaker, asking him to limit his talk in both content and language. (He should be urged *not* to slow down his normal speaking rate, since an important aim of the program is having children listen to authentic native speech.) If he is not a very busy person, you may also ask him to send you a copy of his talk so that you can teach the children some (not all) of the new words. Teach only those words needed to understand the general context.

• The librarian may be asked to prepare a special exhibit in the public library. Sometimes a librarian may be willing to set up a small exhibit of foreign language books in an appropriate place in the language classroom.

• In later stages of learning, when children have started to write, the local printer may be asked to help prepare a brief newspaper with news of the foreign language program.

In communities where there is a large foreign-language-speaking population (and it is to be hoped that the language of this group will be the one you are teaching), it is important that their talents and their resources be tapped to the fullest. Many benefits will accrue to them, to other community members, and to all children from the school's attempt to give these people a feeling of achievement, success, and status.

The cooperation of as many community members as possible should be sought not only to further your language teaching objectives but also to enlist goodwill and support for language teaching programs in general.

Other Devices or Techniques

The Pocket Chart. When reading begins, the pocket chart will be an especially valuable teaching aid. Pocket charts can be bought. (Some sold commercially feature the pocket chart on one side and the flannel board on the other.) Excellent pocket charts can be made very simply, however, by stapling or gluing the bottom and side edges of four or five narrow (about 1½-inch) strips of oaktag to a larger sheet of oaktag. The strips form pockets in which flash cards or pictures can be inserted. For ease in making structural changes, each card should show only one word, punctuation mark, or letter.

The pocket chart can serve many purposes. In addition to its function in developing reading skills, it is extremely effective in dramatizing form or structural changes. For example, at various times during the year, the teacher of French and individual children may stand at the pocket chart which contains the sentence "Il est petit" ("He (It) is small.")

To teach the negative, "il" and "est" would have to be separated and "n'" inserted. "Est" and "petit" would have to be separated and "pas" inserted.

To teach the feminine form, "il" would be removed; "elle" would take its place and the letter "e" would be added to "petit." The reverse could also be done, proceeding from the feminine to the masculine.

To teach the interrogative, the cards for "il" and "est" would be reversed, and a question mark would replace the period.

To teach the "Qui" ("who") form of the interrogative, "Il" would be removed and "Qui" inserted in its place. The question mark would be added.

We could multiply these examples a thousandfold. The *physical* change in the position of the cards which the children make and see has proved very effective in language teaching. The criteria governing the use of the pocket chart are already familiar to us. Many similar examples should be given; only a minimal change should be made. There should be extensive oral practice of the model sentence and of the newly formed sentences. In the elementary schools, still another point is of great importance: The manipulation of the sentences at the pocket chart in the front of the room by the children permits much purposeful movement.

Card materials for use in the chart should be prepared in advance. Manuscript writing is preferable to script for clarity. Cards may be kept in manila envelopes which are clearly labeled. One envelope may contain boys' names; another, girls' names; another, subject pronouns; another, forms of the most common verbs ("be" and "have," for example); another, punctuation marks; others, words within a center of interest, etc.

Charts (sentences or paragraphs) of experiences the children have had or are going to have are also effective when done with the pocket chart. In preparing such experiential stories, you may wish to include pictures. You may place a picture at the end of a sentence to illustrate its content, or you may use a picture in a sentence instead of a word.

It is also advisable to have the children make smaller individual pocket charts of paper or oaktag. Then they can duplicate at their seats the manipulations at the class pocket chart. Moreover, they will be able to create sentences of their own, based on a model the teacher has given, that they can later read to their classmates.

The Vocabulary Wheel. This is another inexpensive device which permits freedom of movement in the classroom while being used to reinforce learning or evaluate progress. A large circle (about 24 inches in diameter) is made of oaktag. Pictures of uniform size are placed at regular intervals on this circle. They are attached to the circle with masking or scotch tape so that removal is easy. The pictures may be related to a central theme or unrelated, for review purposes. On the circle is placed a smaller oaktag circle with a small window, large enough for a picture to show through. In the center, a long paper fastener permits the top circle to spin around so that a picture will appear in the window.

The wheel is spun by a child who either asks questions of his classmates, e.g., "What's this?" or "What color is this?" or tells what he sees. What he sees can be simply the name of the object in a sentence pattern, e.g., "This is a _____" or "I see a _____." In later stages, descriptive and action words can be added, depending on the language items you are emphasizing that day: "I see a small boy." "I see a pretty girl." "The boy is taking the bus."

Picture Dictionaries and Notebooks. Children enjoy making picture dictionaries and picture books related to various centers of interest, e.g., Transportation, Communication, etc. The spiral approach to teaching permits use of the same pictures at numerous times during the year, always in different sentence patterns, e.g.,

> This is a bus.
> This is a red bus.
> This is a big bus.
> This is a big red bus.
> This isn't a bus. It's a car.
> I take the bus in the morning.

As soon as writing begins, the children should be asked to keep neatly labeled notebooks with numbered pages. A table of contents should be kept at the beginning of the notebook. The contents may be listed in terms of centers of interest, e.g., My Classroom; Shopping for Food.

The same cultural situation can be used over and over again to practice newly taught language items. Let us assume that the children have learned and copied an experience chart such as this:

> **EACH DAY**
> I get up at seven o'clock.
> I get washed.
> I get dressed.
> I have my breakfast.
> I leave for school.

At different times during the year, you may turn to the chart and give all kinds of additional practice, using the sentences as a base. For example, change "I" to "he" to "John" to "the boys" to "we," etc. Make the sentences negative ("Say that you don't do these things."). Make the sentences interrogative with "he" as the subject ("Make questions about a boy."). Change the sentences to future ("Say you're going to do these things later.").

Notice that grammatical terminology need not be used. The terms are used only if the children know them from their study of the English language arts. Even if they do, however, the sentences above in parentheses are clearer and more descriptive. You may wish to train children to understand and respond to both the grammatical terminology and the description.

The Blackboard or Chalkboard. Last, but not least—your most important teaching tool, in fact—is the blackboard. Even before children are permitted to see the printed word, the chalkboard can be used by you and the children in a number of ways. Let us list a few of these:

1. From the class data placed at the board, the children can ask and answer questions such as "What class is this?" "How many boys are there in the class?" "Who is absent?" "What is today's date?"

2. In introducing a dialogue, you can sketch stick figures at the board and point to the one who is speaking. Anyone can draw stick figures. A circle for the head, a straight vertical line for the body, and two diagonal lines for the legs are needed, and that is all. Figures can be drawn in a few seconds. The "girl" can have a horizontal line across the vertical line as a symbol for a skirt or a V on her head for a ribbon.

3. In introducing some adjectives or in teaching responses to "How are you?" a circle may be drawn to indicate a head. A mouth line curving up can symbolize "I'm (He's) fine" or "He's happy." A straight line will serve for "I'm fair" or "I'm so-so." A downward curve can mean "I'm ill" or "He's sad," etc. As the question is asked by you or a child, you can elicit the desired response by pointing to one of the three faces.

4. Children may be asked to go to the board to draw something or to add an item to a figure or an object.

5. In teaching time, you may write numbers at the board, e.g., 7:30, 8:15, and study expressions of time in sequence and then at random.

6. You can play many games, e.g., I'm Thinking of a Number.
7. Arithmetic examples can be "read" aloud.
8. In teaching directions or prepositions, you can draw a square to show a park, for example. Various lines can symbolize "around," "through," and "across."
9. At another time, another square may be the symbol for a desk. Heavier chalk marks can symbolize "on," "under," "next to," or "near."
10. Lines can teach "bigger than," "longer than," "shorter than," etc.
11. You may want to have a contest with two teams after you have taught numbers. One child from each team writes a number at the board as you or another child dictates. The same thing can be done later with words.
12. A weather calendar with an umbrella for rain, a sun for good weather, and flakes for snow enables you to practice expressions about weather.
13. A calendar helps you give practice in words and phrases such as "today," "yesterday," "the day before yesterday," etc.
14. Removing a stick figure from a group of three gives practice in questions such as "Who was here?" "How many were there?" "Who went away?"

After reading and writing are begun, the chalkboard can be used in many additional ways. Here are several:

1. The dialogue is written at the board. It is read by teacher, class, and individual children.
2. Action series and conversations are placed at the board.
3. Examples of a grammatical point are placed at the board so that children can see the general pattern, e.g.,

Here	is	my	pen.
Here	is	my	book.

Here	are	my	pen*s*.
Here	are	my	book*s*.

4. Substitution drills are placed at the board, e.g.,

I see the boy.
____ the dog.
____ the cat.
____ the man.

5. More complex substitution drills for extended oral practice and freer expression are placed at the board, e.g.,

Mary	is speaking to the boy.
Mr. Smith	———————— girl.
The boy	———————— dog.
John	———————— teacher.

Children first read the sentences across. Then they can make other combinations.

6. Completion exercises, multiple-choice exercises, and true and false statements are written and read.
7. Homework assignments are written out by several children.
8. Test items are placed at the board.

Of course it is not only by means of the blackboard that the activities above can be carried out. But *every* classroom has a blackboard, whereas some of the other tools mentioned may not be at hand. The chalkboard is always readily available and free from mechanical defects.

The good teacher uses one device one day and another the next to sharpen the children's association between word and concept, to reinforce learning, to ensure comprehension, and to lend needed variety to his teaching.

CORRELATING LANGUAGE AND OTHER CURRICULUM AREAS

As we have presented examples of language activities in the preceding pages, we have touched on some ways in which the study of a foreign language can enrich the child's total school program. In turn, the school curriculum makes valuable contributions to the foreign language program.

In the following pages, we plan to dwell a little more fully on the reciprocal advantages of the program, underscoring some of the statements that have been made and adding or qualifying others. A discussion of correlation is important, since children should be made to feel that learning a language is not something apart from their program, but an integral part of it.

A foreign language program properly administered will develop new skills in a child, increase his knowledge, give him a store of practical and useful information, assist him in establishing desirable work or study habits, and—most important—foster understanding of other people, whether they live in the community or abroad.

The development of skills, habits, knowledge, and attitudes is the goal of all elementary school teaching. Language class activities, geared especially to helping children learn another people's language or customs, assist in developing the attitudes of understanding that are clearly important to both community and national interest.

What can teachers or supervisors do to exploit to the fullest degree the values of foreign language learning? Specific procedures in the suggestions below may need to be adapted or modified to conform to the organization of your school. If the classroom teacher is not the foreign language teacher or the art or music teacher, for example, the suggestions will also require modifications in procedure.

These suggestions are far from complete. They are listed to give experienced teachers more security in their teaching through confirmation of the fact that many things they are doing are done by others in the field and to give new teachers the impetus to explore other avenues of correlation.

1. The foreign language should be used increasingly wherever feasible during the school day.

• Children should be given their names in the foreign language to be used during the day. If there is no equivalent name, one can be chosen from a list.

• Greetings and leave-takings should also be given in the new language.

• Sentences for classroom routines can be introduced gradually during the year. The foreign language can be used in:

a. calling the roll

b. giving the names of absent students

c. counting the boys and girls

d. requesting children to put clothing away or to get it at the end of the day

e. directing children to take out or put away materials they need during all periods

f. assigning housekeeping chores

g. making simple requests: "Go to the board," "Come to the front of the room," "Take this to the office," etc.

h. distributing and collecting materials

i. telling about the weather

j. filling out the weather calendar
   k. giving the day and date
- When writing is begun, the daily class log can be written on the board in the new language. In the beginning, you may repeat the same form of verb ("We will read" or "We will study") for each curriculum area. As the children learn to say and write more, the sentences can increase in complexity.

2. The foreign language will become a functional tool of communication if:
- The various centers of activity in the room are labeled in the foreign language.
- The health chart is translated.
- The monitorial chart is in the foreign language.
- The daily health inspection is conducted in the foreign language.
- Simple arithmetic problems are worked out in the foreign language.
- Geography lessons, not necessarily related to the country whose language they are learning, are given in the foreign language. Simple indications of rivers, mountains, cities (capital, large, small) are often retained more readily if learned in two languages.
- Songs learned in the language class are sung in the assembly and/or taught to other children.
- Dances of the foreign country are learned and enjoyed during the physical education period or the recreation period.
- Simple discussions or directions during the art, music, and health hours are given in the language.
- Pictures, dioramas, and props of all kinds are made during the art period and used in the foreign language period.
- Playlets or skits incorporating the language, songs, dances, etc., of the foreign country are given in the classroom or in the assembly for other classes, parents, or visitors.

3. Supporting activities can be planned for each area of the curriculum to increase understanding of the people whose language is being learned:
- Social studies—committees can do research and prepare reports on various aspects of the foreign culture (history, geography, famous people). They can also study its influence on their own country (past and present).

- Science—discoveries of persons in the foreign country whose work relates to some phase of science being studied by the children can be used as research topics by individuals or committees; reports to the class make a good project.
- English language arts—reading translations of foreign literature at the children's interest and ability level can be assigned. When reading and writing are begun, pen-pal projects may be organized with children who are learning English in other countries. Your children can write in English and ask for replies in the foreign language. You can reverse the procedure when you think it desirable.

It is obvious that the possibilities for correlation in the classrom and in the school are endless. If, moreover, the interrelationship of foreign language and the other curriculum areas is clarified and dramatized for parents and the community, the FLES program will receive the moral and, if necessary, financial support needed for continuation and expansion. Reports of success in one community will serve as a stimulus to other communities.

One way of bringing in parents and the community and of underscoring the fact that foreign language learning fits smoothly into an elementary school program is to plan a program that includes songs, dances, and skits in the foreign language. Letters of invitation may be written in the foreign language and in English, costumes may be made by parent volunteers or the sewing class, scenery may be prepared in the art period, research on the background of the dances may be part of a social studies project, etc. Through such a program, parents and others will see that children can speak another language with facility.

EVALUATING THE PROGRAM—ARTICULATION WITH SECONDARY SCHOOLS

At first glance, it may seem surprising to include testing and articulation in a chapter that has been devoted primarily to games, songs, music, etc. Testing, however, plays a key role in making teaching more effective. It is only by evaluating the growth that children make toward understanding and speaking the language (and later toward reading and writing) that teachers will become aware of the success or failure of their procedures.

Actually, each time a child repeats a sentence or answers a question or dramatizes a conversation, his progress is being "tested." Does a child volunteer an answer? Does he keep the tempo of other class members in choral recitation or in chain drills? The answers to these questions contribute to the teacher's judgment of that child's language ability.

More formal evaluation that points the way toward curriculum revision or improved teaching practices should be written into the curriculum from the very beginning, however. This is true for all curriculum areas. It assumes even more importance in the foreign language program for several reasons:

1. Some people still demand statistical proof of success before they will consider the introduction of foreign languages into their community.

2. Foreign language is a cumulative subject. In order to provide for smooth articulation from the elementary to the secondary schools or to plan the course content for more than one "track" (in cities where there is a full and continuous six- or seven-year program), the secondary schools need to know what the children have already learned. Experience in many cities has shown that secondary school personnel want to see test scores, in addition to the elementary school syllabus. Indeed, in some cities secondary school principals (through their language specialists) ask to participate in the preparation of tests given in the lower school.

3. Since FLES as a general movement is comparatively recent, educators, psychologists, and lay people seek objective data on which to base pleas for more public support, for expanded facilities, for wider teacher training, etc.

4. Colleges will begin training more and more foreign language "majors" or "minors" if they can be sure that statistical evidence of success will create a greater demand for teachers with foreign language competency.

We are all familiar with the many other reasons that warrant assigning to testing an important place in the curriculum.

What kinds of tests are possible in the prereading stage and after reading is introduced? What criteria that are particularly pertinent to foreign languages should guide us in test preparation?

Considerations in Testing In longer, more formal tests, you will find it desirable to:

- Announce all tests in advance.
- Specify their exact scope.

- Make sure that directions are clear. If necessary, give the directions in English.
- Give one or two samples of the answers.
- List the test items according to difficulty, starting with the simpler items.
- Test only what you have practiced thoroughly in class.
- Use different types of stimuli. Use pictures or spoken words or descriptions of situations, and later use written materials.

If the test is given in the sixth or eighth grade just before the child is to be admitted to a secondary school, you may wish to enlist the cooperation of secondary school personnel. They can help to prepare the test items and/or help to decide the passing grade which would determine whether the child should be admitted to the first or second year of language study in the secondary school.

Let us turn our attention to some testing techniques. We have categorized them for convenience only. Obviously, there will be overlapping. Speaking, for example, usually presupposes either listening or reading.

Techniques for Oral and Written Tests *Testing Aural Comprehension.* To test children's ability to understand a complete utterance, the teacher may ask the children to:

1. Carry out a request, e.g., "Go to the door."
2. Carry out a double request, e.g., "Go to the board and write your name."
3. Write or circle numbers, hours, days, and objects on a printed sheet as they are said aloud.
4. Indicate what is being said. The teacher shows two pictures marked "A" and "B," e.g., picture A shows a tall boy; picture B, a short boy. The teacher will say, "The boy is tall." Children write or circle the letter which corresponds.

A prepared tape may also be used for this testing, but first make sure the children are accustomed to its use.

Testing Oral Production. To test some of the skills needed in speaking, the teacher or tape will tell the children to:

1. Repeat sentences of varying lengths, e.g., "John is a boy." "John is that tall boy." "John is that tall boy with brown hair."
2. Direct a question to someone, e.g., "Ask Mary how old she is."
3. Listen to a statement and answer questions about it, e.g., "The red pencil is on the table." "Where is the pencil?" "What color is it?"

4. Answer questions about themselves.
5. Tell what they would ask (or reply) in a situation, e.g., "Someone asks where you are living. What would you say?"
6. Make a statement about a picture or an object.
7. Answer various types of questions, e.g., "Do you like ice cream?" "Begin your answer with 'no.'"
8. Formulate questions based on pictures or statements, e.g., "John is ill." "How is John?" "What is the matter with John?"

Testing Reading Comprehension. To test some of the reading skills, the teacher may ask the children to:
1. Select unrelated words from a group.
2. Place related words under categories.
3. Complete sentences where a choice of three or four words is given.
4. Combine phrases from two columns to make normal utterances.

>How   the book?
>What's   are you?
>Where is   his name?

5. Tell whether a caption under a picture is true or false.
6. Give the correct caption when the one under the picture is false.
7. Read a short paragraph and answer questions about it.
8. Read several sentences about a "situation." Choose the logical response from a list of possible responses.

Testing Writing Ability. To test some skills needed in writing, the teacher may ask the children to:
1. Change a sentence from singular to plural, or affirmative to negative, etc. Grammatical terminology need not be given, as indicated earlier. You may use instead such sentences as "Start the sentence with 'no.'"
2. Fill in or choose a correct form, for example, of the verb or the adjective, e.g., "The boys are (short)." (A change in form is necessary in many foreign languages.)
3. Take a short dictation.
4. Write answers to questions.
5. Write captions for pictures.
6. Make changes in some model sentences necessitated by the use of different time words ("yesterday" or "tomorrow") or different subject pronouns, e.g., "I'm reading. He ___ ___ too."

7. Rewrite a short model composition as though they were talking or telling the story, e.g., "John lives in Paris. He's nine" to "I live in _____. I'm _____."
8. Answer questions about themselves or about a written passage.

Reporting the Achievement of Children Parents, secondary school personnel, and research workers will be interested in the elementary school teacher's evaluation of the child's growth in language. The code used in reporting will vary from community to community, since it will be the code used in evaluating growth in other curriculum areas. Some communities prefer the letters A, B, C, D, and F; some prefer numbers based on the 100 scale; some prefer special symbols, such as E for excellent, S for satisfactory, and P for poor.

You may wish to add a small section on the report card to indicate your evaluation of the child's growth in three basic aspects of language learning: ability to understand; ability to speak; attitudes toward the foreign culture and language study. When reading and writing are begun, comments should also be made about these skills. The terms you will use—"Aural Comprehension" or "Ability to Understand," for example—will depend on the terms you use in other sections of the report card.

Specific notations should also appear on each child's cumulative record card as well as on articulation materials which the elementary school usually sends to the secondary school. Careful reporting not only ensures proper placement of children but also increases the confidence of the secondary schools and the community in the elementary school language program.

SUMMARY

In this chapter, many of the tangibles and some of the intangibles fundamental to teaching or learning a foreign language have been examined. The importance of creating and maintaining a pleasant and yet workmanlike atmosphere in the language class has been stressed.

Several ways were suggested for making the foreign language become another tool of communication for the children, functioning as their native language does. The significance to the class and the community of establishing a cultural island in the classroom was discussed at some length.

Various practices for giving children a feeling of success and achievement and for overcoming the possible reluctance of the community to support FLES have been indicated. Both the climate of the classroom and careful planning by the teacher contribute to the achievement of these goals. Through judicious daily and long-term planning, children can be made to feel that they are continuously growing in their ability to communicate in the foreign language and that language learning is an integral part of the total school curriculum.

In planning for the daily lesson or for the year, the good teacher selects activities that are pleasurable and purposeful in the classroom while leading the children to more habitual control and fluency in the new language. The activities may be chosen from songs, games, practice drills, readings, or dramatizations.

Although one of the objectives of the program is to foster an understanding of the foreign people and their culture in our children, the primary purpose at this level is to teach new communication skills. This objective can be attained by enabling the children to talk about everyday school and community experiences in the new language. Children will gain an appreciation of the foreign culture as they listen to and speak the language of native speakers of that culture. Language and culture are inseparable; thus the development of skill in one leads automatically to the development of appreciation of the other.

In order to gain public support and enlist the cooperation of parents, it is desirable to involve the parents and other community members in the program. This is particularly the case when the language being taught is spoken by some of the people living in the community.

As a further means of enlisting community support and giving children a continuous foreign language program articulated with the secondary schools, formal measures of evaluation should be cooperatively evolved. We have suggested several techniques for doing this.

Here and in preceding chapters, we have indicated that effective teaching of foreign languages results from careful but flexible planning, from a multiplicity of approaches, and from the selection of one or more language-producing activities. Above all, it results from the desire and willingness of the teacher to adapt or create techniques or materials that are based on his knowledge of his own strengths and resources, those of the children, and those of the school and community.

It is in this way only that teaching a foreign language becomes a science and an art—both essential sides of the same coin.

6

How Should Materials Be Prepared?

INTRODUCTION

Since many school systems will prefer to prepare their own guide for teaching foreign languages, a detailed analysis of the procedures involved is presented here. The roles various persons should play and the processes that need to be considered in the production of a useful guide are the subject of this chapter.

Both supervisors and teachers play important roles in the language teaching program. The organization of classes, time schedules, assignment of teachers, purchase of materials, articulation with the secondary school, and community cooperation—all are the particular province of the supervisor, but all concern the classroom teacher as well. The curriculum, considered in its broad sense—all the experiences children engage in both in and out of school in the achievement of educational goals—is in the domain of the teacher, but is of deep concern to the supervisor. It is obvious that collaboration between supervisors and teachers in the preparation of the foreign language guide is eminently desirable.

Supervisors and teachers should make or accept several basic assumptions before starting to write or adapt materials. Also there are definite criteria evolved by persons engaged in such work against which materials of instruction should be checked. This chapter will outline these briefly.

BASIC ASSUMPTIONS

Preparation of Instructional Materials Is a Cooperative Effort
Since language teaching draws upon the knowledge or methods of several disciplines—linguistics, psychology, anthropology—the materials should be written or at least discussed regularly by a committee, and not by one person alone. The committee should consist of people who each bring special knowledge and insights to group deliberations.

A native of the country whose language will be taught should be on the committee, for example. The native speaker will perform three major roles:

1. He will bring insight into the customs, mores, and values of his country.

2. He will assist the writers in identifying and pointing up the contrasts and the similarities between his native language and English.

3. He will check the materials (dialogues, drills, etc.) for authenticity and accuracy, both linguistic and psychological.

The committee should include several classroom teachers, at least one of whom has a knowledge of the foreign language. Teachers are in an ideal position to indicate desirable and logical points of correlation with the other curriculum areas at each level. Suggestions related to the cultural topics or centers of interest for each level should certainly evolve from their contributions to committee discussions. The topics may, in turn, determine the placement or reintroduction of items of structure and the vocabulary to be presented or reinforced. The classroom teachers can also recommend projects or culminating activities that will bring together knowledge or skills in several curriculum areas. They also know how much content their pupils can absorb in a given period of time and the types of classroom activities that are usually pleasurable to children and therefore successful.

Another person on the committee should know something about the nature of language and language learning. If no one on the school staff meets these requirements and if the supervisor does not consider this area of knowledge his strong point, he may wish to enlist the cooperation of the neighboring high school, college, or state-education-department staff. Doing so may be an added safeguard only, however, since close adherence to the linguistic principles outlined throughout this book should result in a most acceptable curriculum guide.

If the language is taught in one or more neighboring secondary schools, it is desirable—in fact, essential—to invite several language teachers from that school to participate. Such representation will ensure smooth articulation for the pupils and continuity without frustration for the secondary school teachers.

Approach Is "Linguistic" The approach to language teaching should be based on the findings of linguistic science about which there is general agreement among educators. The method or approach that avails itself of these findings is known by several names: "aural-oral," "audio-lingual," "audio-oral," and "audio-visual." All—with only slight variation between them—are based on the principles outlined in Chapter 2. They are restated here briefly where they apply specifically to the preparation of instructional materials.

- Language is a system of arbitrary vocal sounds and sound sequences which all the speakers in a community use to communicate and to interact.
- Speech is primary. Writing and, therefore, reading are secondary representations of speech.
- "Language" means the authentic spoken language of the community.
- A knowledge of the spoken language of a community is gained by recording and describing what the native speakers actually say. It is not gained by reading what a grammarian thinks they should say.
- Language learning assumes the formation of new habits of speech and thought.

Implications of These Assumptions. What are some of the implications drawn from these principles that will affect the preparation of materials?

- The *sound system* of the language—many call it "the stream of speech"—should be given priority in teaching. Sounds and sound sequences should not be taught in isolation—particularly with young children—but in normal speech, with normal intonation, rhythm, pauses, and stresses.

Provision should be made for the systematic reintroduction in normal speech situations of the same intonation, stress, rhythm, and sequence of sounds.

Provision should also be made for the early teaching, the varied but intensive practice, and the constant reintroduction of features of the sound system that may cause difficulty because they conflict with those found in English. The younger the child, however, the less the difficulty caused by the ingrained speech habits of the native language will be.

- Since language has system, pupils should be helped to acquire that system. This is accomplished in several ways: (1) by giving them numerous examples of a feature of form or word order (*always* in a real communication situation); (2) by providing varied but intensive practice in hearing and saying the new item (in dialogues, play activities, talks, drills, games and songs, for example); (3) by making sure that the feature of form or word order recurs regularly in later lessons; and (4) by combining it in later lessons with other logical words or language patterns which the children have learned.

When a language item causes difficulty because it is totally or partially dissimilar to the English equivalent, it should be given extra emphasis by means of additional systematic practice and reintroduction of the item at frequent intervals. With older children, the contrast with English may be pointed out or elicited. When this is done, the analysis or comparison should be brief, and it should be in descriptive terms only.

- Many repetitions of material are necessary to ensure learning. General suggestions concerning reintroduction of materials have been given above. In addition, directions for teachers should indicate specifically the number and kinds of repetition needed in introducing any new item.

- The language items featured in the materials should be authentic —items which children of the same age group would use in talking about similar happenings or situations in their country.

- The situations in which language is introduced and practiced should be real to the children. They like to talk about themselves, their families, their friends, their hobbies and pets, and their homes and communities.

- Choice of activities should be based on the children's age and interests; teachers know, from their experience with children in the English language arts and other programs, what kinds of activities result in listening or speaking participation.

- Conversations and interchanges lend themselves to the practice of language in authentic situations. Many brief dialogues that are useful at various grade levels should be included in the guide.

- Since it is desirable that pupils attain reasonable mastery of the sound system *before* they start to read, directions to teachers should emphasize and list varied aural-oral activities that will help sustain interest during the prereading stage.

- The specific materials that will be used when the transition from the audio-oral stage to the reading stage is made should be indicated. Not all the material used in the prereading stage can or should be used.
- At the beginning level, the sound and structure systems of the new language should receive more attention than its vocabulary. Nevertheless, enough vocabulary should be introduced so that the children will have something to talk about in real situations, so that sounds and structure can be presented and practiced in sentences having real meaning, and so that the dialogues will have an authentic ring.

Several things should be avoided, however. These are (1) following any word list slavishly, (2) giving the children all the words revolving around a center of interest in any one year, and (3) making children or parents feel that the acquisition of vocabulary is the most important part of language learning.

- Vocabulary for *active* use should be introduced gradually and in sentence patterns with which the children are already familiar.

Much of the vocabulary in the dialogues and stories will be "passive," introduced primarily to make the material sound natural. Children will understand the meaning of the words; they will be able to use them when dramatizing the dialogue, for example, but they will not be expected to use them in creating new sentences or conversations.

Vocabulary items for active use should be starred in the curriculum guide and used by teachers in the presentation and practice of new structures. The active items should be reinserted in as many dialogues, situations, and activities as possible throughout the grades.

The unit in which the vocabulary item first appears should be indicated as a reminder of the original context or center of interest. A sentence including the vocabulary item would be helpful. The word "cold," for example, can have many meanings, depending upon the context. ("The soup is cold," "I have a cold," "He's cold.") The unit number and an example of the word used in context will help teachers determine (1) the meaning of the word which can be used in any reintroduction of it, (2) the new meanings of the word which need to be taught, if any, (3) the unit in which children are ready to practice the contrasts in meaning, e.g., in French, Spanish, or Italian, "He's cold" and "The soup is cold."

- Grammar is not generally analyzed in the lower grades in the elementary schools. The focus is on grammar in use rather than on grammatical analysis or terminology. Children gain insight into the pattern of structure through the numerous examples they hear and say. Children, however, should be helped to "see" the recurring pattern or system. After forms of words related to one structure or grammatical item have been presented separately, they should be practiced together. For example, combination practice should be given in all the personal pronouns of a verb tense or all the forms of an adjective (masculine and feminine, singular and plural). In this way children develop an understanding of the system of the language.

In the upper grades, when children ask about the use or distribution of a structure or form, a brief descriptive explanation should be given. For example, if the question is about the past tense, the teacher would say, "We use this form with words such as 'yesterday' or 'last night.'" Since few simple, descriptive grammars are available, the curriculum guide may include brief descriptive statements of the structures that are introduced in each grade.

If your elementary school includes the seventh and eighth grades and children are going into a secondary school where they will continue their language study, it is imperative to ascertain what the receiving school expects in the way of preparation in grammar. It goes without saying that children should be able to meet the requirements of the secondary school.

Language Study Is an Integral Part of the Total Curriculum
The language program should contribute to the objectives and learnings of the elementary school program. In turn, it should be enriched by the contributions which the other subject areas can make to it. Possibilities of correlation of subject matter in each grade should be carefully explored. A school-wide activity such as a fair, a fiesta, or a play may utilize information and skills from every area of the curriculum, as indicated in earlier chapters. In addition, the guide should indicate specific places in each curriculum area where the children may further use some skill or knowledge in the foreign language. For example, songs in the new language may be used in the physical education or music period; simple mathematical drills may be conducted in the language; social studies research may center about an aspect of the culture of the other country or a pen-pal project may be initiated; games in the physical education period may be the games played by children in the for-

eign land. Needless to say, there are numerous possibilities for enrichment.

Methodology Is Derived from Many Sources Although language learning demands that the teacher use many specific techniques, they are used in the context of elementary school philosophy and practices, which are based on knowledge gained from decades of observation and study of young children. In addition to the special teaching skills needed in foreign language teaching, the teacher should have an appreciation of the characteristics of children at different age levels, of the importance of readiness and habit formation, of the children's mental health needs, of the numerous techniques for creating and maintaining interest, and of the favorable effects of reward and success.

The guide should reflect an understanding of the elementary school philosophy and the new concept of culture, which we owe to the anthropologists. This understanding will be apparent in the treatment of the classroom environment, experiences for children of different groups, varied activities leading to habit formation and to cultural insight, and the progressively more complex language and cultural concepts appropriate for each grade.

Evaluation Takes Place at Every Step The term "evaluation" has several important aspects. Two are of immediate concern in curriculum construction; they are related to the experimental nature of the guide and to the language testing program.

As is the case with other curriculum areas, the FLES program should never be considered definitive. The first guide may fail the test of actual classroom practice. Moreover, the dynamic character of language and the tremendous upsurge of interest in language may mean that today's thinking will need modification tomorrow. The underlying philosophy—and hence the elementary school curriculum—may undergo changes that will necessitate emphasizing or deemphasizing points of correlation.

The teachers who are using the guide should be asked to submit recommendations for its improvement at regular intervals. A committee should be asked to evaluate these recommendations and incorporate them in revisions of the guide as soon as feasible.

Although the primary emphasis in FLES should be on teaching and not on testing, provision for objective testing should be built into the guide from the outset. The testing program, as we know, serves many purposes. It can point up needs for curriculum revision, different materials, or improved or modified teaching techniques. A testing program may demonstrate that insufficient progress is being made in one or another language skill or that the content is either not enough or too much.

In the sphere of language teaching, where continued community acceptance and support are of vital interest, it is essential to be able to report progress accurately. The guide should contain general principles of informal and more formal test construction, simple test items, and perhaps one or two model tests.

DECISIONS AND RESPONSIBILITIES

When agreement has been reached on the principles that will underlie the guide, two questions should be thoroughly discussed before writing is begun: (1) In which grade will language be introduced? (2) What will the objectives of the program be? For example, will the course be purely audio-oral? If not, when will reading be introduced? Will writing be introduced? If so, when? Will the teaching of some aspects of culture be systematic, or should they be the incidental outcome of activities such as festivals or games?

The answers to these and other basic questions will determine important features of the guide, such as the amount of language content recommended for each grade (Will we still want to include all the structures previously agreed upon, even if we plan a three-year instead of a four-year course?), the types of activities recommended for each year, the suggestions to teachers concerning the transition to reading and writing. The decisions you make should be based on your intimate knowledge of your students, your community, and yourselves. It is, of course, desirable to examine the literature concerning these questions, but two basic points to remember are these: (1) There is no one right answer to any of these questions; and (2) what works in Scanville may not be wholly suitable in your situation.

It *is* important that the point of view which determined the content of the guide be clearly stated at the outset, that the rationale be indicated, and that each step in the guide be a reflection of the adopted point of view.

After decisions on such important questions as grade of introduction have been reached, committee assignments should be made, depending upon the number of people who are participating and their areas of specialization and interest. In general, it would be desirable for everyone on the committee to examine the important literature in the field. All could read one or two recommended texts or guides, or individual members could each read and summarize one for the entire group.

Production assignments should be on an individual basis, but evaluation of each phase should be a cooperative undertaking. A chairman or secretary should collate materials, set dates for meetings, arrange for duplicating the materials, and do the hundred other chores that go into a good finished product.

Committee members should:

- Write to government agencies such as the U.S. Department of Health, Education, and Welfare and to language teachers' associations such as the Modern Language Association, asking for available materials. (See Sources and Resources for Teachers.)
- Ask other school systems for their foreign language curriculum guides. You will find them very generous in sharing materials. Names of school systems that have prepared guides are found in the bibliographies listed in Sources and Resources for Teachers.
- Study curriculum guides for other subjects taught in the school or district.
- Prepare a list of structures to be taught throughout the entire program.
- Draw up a list of vocabulary items in each topic for the entire program.
- Determine the cultural topics or centers of interest through which the structures and the vocabulary will be presented and practiced.
- Decide on the best method of giving children insight into the foreign culture and draw up a list of items for the teacher, e.g., When do foreign children go to school? When do foreign children have holidays? What games do they like? What toys do they have? Do they keep pets?
- Divide the topics and language items into grades or levels.
- Arrange them in logical order.
- Plan a list of activities for listening alone; for listening and speaking; for listening, speaking, and reading; for listening, speaking, and writing.
- Provide suggestions for broad culminating activities such as assembly programs, festivals, plays, trips.

After this preliminary research and listing of materials, additional discussion will be needed, since again there is no *one* answer to the following problems:

What Should Be the Format of the Guide? The decision may well depend upon an existing format for another subject area that has found favor with the teachers. You may, however, wish to consider several possibilities:

1. The material to be taught in each year is contained in several *descriptive* units that the teacher will be expected to divide into daily or weekly teaching lessons. Each unit includes (*a*) the cultural topic in dialogue, story, play, or other form, (*b*) the language items (sounds, structure, and vocabulary) to be singled out for emphasis (illustrated in complete sentences), (*c*) the activities (drills, games, songs, etc.) for approaching the unit and giving practice, and (*d*) a possible culminating activity.

2. The material—the cultural topic in dialogue or story form and the language items for intensive practice—is divided into several descriptive units. In this format, however, the procedures and the practice activities for the entire year are listed at the back of the guide. (This method will present no disadvantage to the eager and alert teacher, who will choose the appropriate activities for each language item to be taught.)

3. The material is presented in chart form. The division may be by week, month, or cultural topic. One cultural topic may be used for a week, for several weeks, or even for months. One column contains a suggested social situation or cultural topic, e.g., going to the store; a second, structural items; a third, vocabulary. Activities may be listed in a fourth column. You may wish to add a fifth column for the outcomes to be achieved, but this is really unnecessary. In this format, general outcomes are discussed in the introduction and the specific outcomes are obvious from the listing in the first three columns of the cultural topic and the language items to be emphasized. In a format of this kind, dialogues, stories, and plays are grouped together in another section.

4. Another arrangement, but one that requires hours of work, is division of the materials into daily lesson units. An excellent example of this type of format is the Margit McRae text, *Teaching Spanish in the Grades.*

The format may be a combination of any of the above. A chart followed by sample units or lessons is always useful. Whatever format is agreed upon, it should be clearly indicated and followed consistently. If a separate guide is being prepared for each grade level, some uniformity should be maintained for the three- or four-year series.

What Approach Should Be Recommended to Teachers? As noted in Chapter 4, several approaches are possible. This fact should be emphasized in the directions for teachers. No matter which initial approach has been used in any unit, it is desirable to include one or more dialogues, stories, songs, games, etc. Teachers should be given specific guidance in preparing and using normal conversational exchanges, questions and responses, and longer extended dialogues.

How Much New Material Should Be Introduced Each Year? The answer will depend, of course, upon the number of hours per week devoted to language study and the abilities of the pupils. Some school systems have found, however, that the average child at the beginning level, when language is started in grade 3, is able to learn approximately two hundred active words and twenty structures. The amount can be increased each year. It is important to point out that the *number* of language items to be covered should not be a source of major concern. The children's ability to use the structures they have learned with meaning and pleasure in a variety of contexts is more essential.

What Should Be the Sequence of the Material? Again, there is no one answer! In general, as far as cultural situations are concerned, the *here* and *now* should precede references to places in the country of the "target" language. This does not mean that reference to the foreign country (its games, songs, holidays) must be deferred for any definite length of time. It does mean that—since our primary purpose is to teach children to communicate in another medium—we must make it possible for them to talk about holidays or events within their experience. Moreover, any reference to events or holidays in the foreign land should be preceded by a discussion of customs with which the children are familiar. Only by association with a known event can the new cultural knowledge become meaningful.

The principle of starting with the "here and now" also assumes that the children will learn first to talk about themselves—their classroom, their school, and their homes. They will then talk about the neighborhood in which they live. In ever-widening circles, we will help them reach out to the broader community and then to the foreign land.

In helping pupils talk about themselves in their environment, we make them aware of children of their own age in the foreign country through constant reference to their life and customs. The point of departure for the comparison should always be the child himself and the environment with which *he* is familiar.

It is important that language items be grouped together in a logical sequence. For example, after teaching "How are you?" you may prefer to teach "How is your father?" or "What's your father's name?" since you have undoubtedly taught "What's your name?" You may, however, prefer to teach "Where do you live?" rather than "How is your father?" or "What's your father's name?" Any one of the three sequences would be as "right" as any other one, provided that the new structure is built on familiar material and that children are helped to see its importance in normal communication.

The dialogues or stories throughout the units may all be centered around the activities of several children of one family or of a group of friends. On the other hand, materials need not be related in any way as far as story line or unifying theme is concerned. It has been our experience, however, that children prefer to hear about the adventures of boys and girls they have long been acquainted with and with whom they can learn to identify themselves.

MINIMUM ESSENTIALS

Since teachers who will be called upon to teach language may not be language experts and since FLES is a comparatively new phenomenon, the guide should be fuller than one designed for another area. It should be divided by grades (3, 4, 5, 6, 7, 8) or by levels, with a clear explanation of "level" in the introduction. All the grades or levels may be contained in one guide, or you may prefer separate guides for each grade or level.

The following minimum essentials should be included in the guide for each grade or level:

1. A clear statement of objectives. What abilities, skills, information, and attitudes are hoped for? To what degree will the children be expected to acquire them?

2. An uncluttered chart listing the specific language items and cultural topics for each year.

3. Division of content. The division may be based on the cultural unit (the center of interest), the completion of which may take a week, a month, or more. Or it may be based on language items, with suggestions of areas of living or cultural units in which their use would be most natural.

At each level after the first, it would be most desirable to give a brief résumé of the language items and centers of interest taught at the preceding level. Since reinforcement through repetition is desirable, teachers will use items from the previous year's work in warm-up periods, new dialogues, recombined dialogues or reading passages, and practice activities.

4. Numerous examples of activities which could be used in presenting or practicing language items. In addition, several detailed illustrations of procedures which are especially useful in the language class should be included. One may show the step-by-step procedure through which a specific dialogue is presented for comprehension; another, the steps in helping children dramatize the dialogue; another, the teaching of a song or dance; another, the modeling and repetition of a word, expression, or structure; another, the practice of a specific language item through a question-and-answer technique or substitution drill.

5. A time schedule for a fifteen- to twenty-minute language period. The following schedule, an elaboration of one suggested previously, may be helpful to teachers:

Warm-up (five minutes)—simple questions and answers about the weather and absent children, homework, the recitation of previously learned material (a dialogue, a song), a chain drill.

Presentation of new material (five minutes)—motivation, statement of aim by the teacher, review of related material on which the new item or dialogue or story is based. The *new* material may be the introduction of a new dialogue, two or four lines of the new dialogue or of a dialogue previously introduced, a structure, a group of vocabulary items within the center of interest, a new type of drill—the Directed Practice Drill, for example.

Practice activities (five minutes) [1]—language drills such as chain practice, questions and answers, pattern practice, etc.

---

[1] When the language period is longer, more time should be devoted to this section.

Songs, games, or dramatizations of known dialogue or story (five minutes).

6. Language items in complete sentences or in normal utterances in each unit. (Please remember that "Yes, of course" and "Why?" are utterances.) It may be desirable to include a simple phonetic [2] transcription of each new sentence or utterance and each vocabulary item. Intonation and stress should also be marked. The marking of the sound system should be *simply* explained with illustrations.

7. An exhaustive list of clearly defined activities for inducing language practice. It is better to suggest ten activities for practicing one item than to have the teacher feel at a loss.

8. Vocabulary in a cultural topic. This should be carefully delimited. If the cultural setting is the home, for example, teachers should be guided in their choice of the one or two aspects of home living that will be discussed in that grade and the appropriate vocabulary. The points of comparison or contrast with the same aspect of home living in the foreign culture should also be indicated. For example, in learning how to talk about getting up or going to bed, the children may be told and taught how to say "French children usually go to bed at _____ o'clock."

9. Pronunciation drills for situations in which special intensive pronunciation practice is needed.

10. Short, authentic dialogues built around each cultural situation. There should be two or three formal dialogues for each unit, if possible. One dialogue may introduce the area of living and language items, another longer dialogue may employ these same concepts and language items with other themes, and another may use the language items in combination with previously learned items or topics.

Preceding each dialogue, there should be several English sentences that the teacher would use in explaining the situation or setting to the children. For example, "Henry meets Paul on the street. Paul admires Henry's dog. He wants to play with him."

The dialogues should contain about six to eight sentences or utterances and should be written so that there will be a logical break after every two sentences. The two sentences can be practiced in chain and other types of drills or informal dramatizations.

---

[2] The International Phonetic Alphabet system (IPA) will be useful in marking the broad phonetic features of new words, utterances, and sentences.

Only two or three speakers should be used at the very beginning. Some writers recommend that the dialogue for all speakers be about the same length. If the reverse-role technique (see Chapter 4) is used, however, the number of utterances per speaker should not really matter. (See Sample Materials for dialogues.)

11. Well-known, simplified children's stories. Those with repetitive motifs such as The Three Bears or The Pig Who Wouldn't Go over the Stile are particularly good. They may be recorded by a native speaker.

12. Reading materials (narrative passages) which recombine the known language items from dialogues or conversations.

13. A section with brief structural and pronunciation notes (for the *teacher's* use only). The terminology should be as simple as possible. New technical terms if used should be defined, and illustrative examples should be given.

14. A list of songs accompanied by simple music.

15. A list of language games.

16. A suggested list of visual materials (flash cards, lotto games, pictures, flannel board, magnetic board, etc.).

17. A vocabulary and structure list of all the items in the *entire* program in alphabetical order, indicating the *year* and the *unit* in which the item was introduced. You may also prefer to give a sentence (taken from a dialogue or story) for each item, illustrating its use in a familiar context. Vocabulary items for active use should be starred so that the teacher will reintroduce them as frequently as possible.

18. Techniques and sample test items for evaluating children's growth in language ability.

19. Examples of culminating activities in which other community members or parents could participate.

20. A list of sources of materials—where to buy recordings or props, where to procure free materials, where to find simple reading materials, for example.

21. Recommended reading for teachers—magazines, professional journals, texts, guides, brochures.

A CHECKLIST FOR CURRICULUM WRITERS

You may want to ask yourselves some of these questions about your first draft. Many others will occur to you as you examine them and consider your school and community situation as realistically as possible.

1. Have we started with the "here and now" of our school and community, so that children will realize that they can talk about the things they have always talked about—but in another language?

2. Have we introduced concepts of customs and values of the foreign country, associating them with concepts that are within the experience of our children?

3. Have we used a *cyclical* or *spiral* approach? Do the same language items reoccur many times in new contexts or in combination with other contexts in dialogues, reading selections, and language practice exercises? Is the same cultural topic or center of interest studied at each succeeding level or grade in greater depth, with extended vocabulary and more complex structures?

4. Have we presented very little new material at one time, thus permitting the children to gain a firm grasp of each new item?

5. Have we made the instructions to the teachers clear and definite?

6. Have we given many examples of "how to present" and "how to practice"?

7. Have we demonstrated how recordings, visits, games, and puppet shows can "produce" language?

8. Have we indicated points of correlation with other areas of the elementary school curriculum?

9. Have we provided for evaluation of the program?

10. Have we taken into consideration the language program in the secondary school which our pupils may attend?

11. Have we made provision for continued and extensive audio-oral work, even after reading and writing are introduced?

12. Have we demonstrated how listening, speaking, and later, reading and writing activities are integrated in real communication, so that children and teachers will realize that the new language—like English—is used to talk about, read about, and write about things that people everywhere normally talk about, read about, and write about?

SUMMARY

Working together as a team, many persons should prepare the curriculum and the accompanying instructional materials for the FLES program. A native speaker, several classroom teachers, secondary school staff members, and wherever possible, a person with a knowledge of linguistics should cooperate in the development of a curriculum.

All members of the committee should agree on the philosophy which underlies the materials. The principles which guided the committee in preparing the curriculum should be clearly explained in its introduction and reflected throughout the guide.

Since this area of teaching is comparatively new, the guide for teachers should be written in great detail. Sources of help to teachers should be clearly indicated, as well as specific activities and procedures that will be useful in the development of each of the language skills.

It has been our experience in many years of teaching, supervising, and observing that teachers do *not* consider a detailed guide a straitjacket. Beginning teachers appreciate extensive support until they are able to expand or create on their own; experienced or creative teachers may choose from the long array of suggestions some technique they may not have tried and, even more important, find confirmation in the guide of procedures or devices they have used intuitively. In any case, it is always better to err on the side of too much rather than too little.

Sample Materials

Although teachers like to find concrete illustrations of materials in a text of this type, this section is included only with hesitation. There is always the problem of omitting excellent materials or of giving the impression that those included are recommended as models to be followed. There are many fine materials in this area, but space limitations confine us to one or two representative samples and material the author has prepared.

In reviewing these sample materials, remember that all material should be adapted to fit your personality; your children's age, ability, and interest levels; your school and your community.

Several examples of brief conversational exchanges and longer dialogues under several topics are included merely to indicate what is possible in preparing such material. These, as well as all other materials, need adaptation based on the language being studied, the learning level, the age and interests of the children, the community, etc. You may wish to refer to pages 119 to 120 of Chapter 5 for illustrations of ways in which new sentences may be added to basic conversations at each succeeding learning level.

In the commercially prepared materials, you will find a preponderance of French and Spanish materials, since French and Spanish are the two languages most frequently taught in the elementary school. Selected materials and procedures may be adapted for the other languages.

Sample Materials

DIALOGUES

IDENTIFICATION

A. Good morning. What's your name?
It's John. What's yours?
Mary.

B. Hello, Joan. Today is my birthday.
Really? How old are you?
I'm ten.

C. What does your father do?
He's a policeman.

D. This is a picture of my family. Look. This is my sister.
What's her name?
Rose. She's two years old.
Does she talk yet?
Of course. She talks all the time.

PETS

That's a nice dog. What's his name?
It's Danny.
Can I play with him sometime?
Sure. Come to my house this afternoon.
Thanks. I'll ask my mother. I'll see you later.

THE SCHOOL

A. Where's the library?
It's on the third floor.

B. Are you going to be in the play?
What play?
The one they're giving in the assembly tomorrow.

C. Are you coming on the trip on Saturday?
Of course. Are you taking your lunch?
Yes. Are you?
I am too.

D. Who is the new principal?
I think his name is Mr. Jones.

E. Did you do your social studies homework last night?
Yes. Why?
We have to give our committee report today.
I'm ready. I have some maps and these pictures too.
They look interesting.

THE HOME

A. What time do you have breakfast?
We always have breakfast at eight.
Even on Sunday?
Yes. On Sunday too.

B. Where do you study?
I usually study in the living room.

C. Do you watch television every night?
Oh, no. My mother won't let me.

D. Put on your new suit, Paul.
Do I have to, Mother?
Yes. Aunt Barbara is coming to visit us.
When is she coming?
She'll be here soon.
Are we going to have apple pie?
Yes. And vanilla ice cream too.
Good. I'll get dressed right away.

SHOPPING

A. May I have that balloon?
Which one?
The red one, over there.

B. Do you sell lollipops?
Of course. What flavor do you want?
Lemon, please.

C. Please let me have a pound of cookies.
Anything else?
No, thank you. That's all.

D. I have to go to the stationery store. Do you want to come with me?
What do you have to buy?

Sample Materials

A ruler and a compass.
I can lend you mine.
Thanks, but I want to buy my own. I need them in math every day.

ILLNESS

A. What's the matter with you?
   I have a stomachache.

B. How do you feel today?
   Better, thank you.

C. Why were you absent?
   I had a cold.

D. Good morning, Johnny.
   Good morning, Doctor.
   What hurts you, Johnny?
   Everything. I hurt all over.
   Let me see your tongue. Mm. What did you eat last night?
   Some chocolate cake.
   How many pieces?
   Only four.

OTHER MATERIALS

EN FRANCE (UNIT 1) [1]

Vocabulary

Bonjour, mes enfants.
Bonjour, Mademoiselle, (Madame, Monsieur).
Au revoir.
Bravo!

Recommended props are:
1. A map of France (a must) and a map of the world.
2. A small French flag.
3. A small American flag.
4. A small piece of silk material.
5. A small piece of woolen material.

[1] You may wish to begin teaching the language in this way.
M. Devaux and M. Finocchiaro, *Mes Amis François et Sophie*, Regents Publishing Co., New York, 1965.

6. 1 or 2 artificial flowers.
   7. Cut-outs: 3 black piles of coal
                a bunch of grapes (red or white)
                1 ship
                a buffalo or a horse
   8. Crayons (red and blue) for each child.

General Notes The first unit should be devoted to a talk about France. It should not exceed two periods. The maps should be on the wall or resting on the chalk tray. The map of France should be a very simple map with no words. Only the borders, the Seine and Loire rivers, a few peaks for the Alps and the Pyrenees should be indicated. In fact, you may wish to duplicate the map in the children's book omitting the drawings.

You should start a "coin français" where anything related to France could be displayed for a while: cut-out pictures of landscapes or typical buildings (Le Louvre), dolls, souvenirs of travel (pottery, ash-trays, lace, etc.). Stamps and coins can make an attractive board. The children themselves could prepare it.

If there are several French classrooms in the school, you may wish to exchange interesting items. You may even wish to organize contests with other teachers, e.g., illustrations of the Christmas of François and Sophie, of the action verbs, of the different expressions of illnesses. These projects should be prepared at home by the children or perhaps during the art period.

Procedure As you enter the classroom or start the French period, greet the children with a clear and loud "Bonjour, mes enfants," and as you proceed to your desk, turn to them and say, "Do you know what language I was just speaking? It wasn't English, was it? I'm not going to let you guess. I was speaking French. . . . You know French is a beautiful language and we're going to learn to speak it together. It will be easy. . . . Do you want to know what you have to do? Just listen to me carefully and repeat when I tell you to repeat. You'll see, it will be fun. . . . Let's try!

"When I came in, I said, 'Bonjour, mes enfants.' "

"What do you think I was saying? . . . Listen again. 'Bonjour, mes enfants.' "

"What should you answer me—'Bonjour, mes enfants'? . . . Of course not, you wouldn't say 'Good morning, children,' you will say, 'Bonjour, Mademoiselle (Madame, Monsieur).' Let's try that together.

... 'Bonjour, Mademoiselle (Madame, Monsieur).' All right ... now let's repeat the whole thing. I'll pretend I'm coming in." (Go back to the door.) "Bonjour, mes enfants."
"Bonjour, Mademoiselle."
"Let's practice that."
"Bonjour, Mademoiselle."
"Did you see how easy it was? Do you know that you already know many French words? . . . Yes" (nod your head firmly). "Suppose your Dad is taking your Mother out tonight. . . . He first gets the car out of the . . . what? . . . The garage. There you are! 'Garage' is a French word. . . . And then, they drive to the restaurant. . . . 'Restaurant' is another French word. They sit down; on the table, there is a nice bouquet. . . . 'Bouquet' is also a French word! Your mother asks for the menu. . . . There you are again, 'menu' is a French word, too. . . . Then she says, 'Oh, I'd like some hors d'oeuvres to start with.' 'Hors d'oeuvres' is a French word. It means appetizers. How many of these words did you know? . . . You see, I was right when I told you that you knew French words already. And I'm sure we will discover a lot more as we learn the language together.

"Do you know where French is spoken? . . . French is spoken in France of course, but it is spoken also in Canada, here" (show on the world map) "in some Caribbean Isles and even in our own country, around New Orleans.

"Do you know why French is spoken in these places? . . . I am sure that you have heard of some of the famous French people who crossed the Atlantic a long time ago . . ." (Elicit or give the following) "Jacques Cartier explored the St. Lawrence River. Of course, you heard about him . . . And Champlain . . . We have a beautiful lake in the State of New York. . . . And do you remember the name of that great French friend of George Washington? Yes! Lafayette. He came over here from France to help us during the War of Independence.

"Well, you see, you know French words and also famous French people. Now let's talk a little about France. Let's have a look at it on this map. You know it's located in Europe and it's slightly smaller than the State of Texas. I'm sure you know the name of the capital. What is it? . . . Yes! Paris, of course. . . . Where is it located on the map? . . . Here it is! Let's have this little flag of three colors, blue, white, red, pinned at the right place to show us where the capital is." (Child is sent to attach the flag.) "Do you know anyone who has been to Paris? Tell us about it." (Children tell about family or friends.)

"Well, let's mark a few big cities in the same way. Look! Here I have a ship. It is for Marseille because Marseille is the largest sea-port in France. It's down here, on the Mediterranean Sea. Will you pin it here, please?" (Child does so.)

"Now! I have a small piece of silk material. It is for Lyon, the city where they make a lot of silk material and where they raise silkworms. Will you pin the silk at Lyon, please?" (Child does so.) "By the way, Lyon is also the birthplace of the French Punch and Judy show. They call it 'Guignol,' and you know, the French children love it just as you enjoy your puppet shows.

"Now look! I have a small piece of wool and three heaps of coal. We'll use them to represent Lille, up in the north. There are a lot of mills in Lille weaving fabrics of wool and, not very far, very important coal mines.

(Pick up the grapes.) "Well, what do I have here? Yes! Grapes. Where do you think I am going to put them? I could put them in different places, but we'll pin them near the city where they grow the most grapes, Bordeaux . . . Here, near the Atlantic Ocean. . . . When you go to France, all around Bordeaux, you will see miles and miles of vineyards.

"I have just one little thing left: a few flowers. Do you have any idea which city they are going to represent? . . . Well, it's a beautiful city, near Italy. This city is called Nice. Here you will find fields and fields of flowers covering the slopes near the sea: roses, carnations, mimosa . . . All kinds of flowers. . . . There you are, for Nice.

"Now let's say the names of the cities in French: repeat them after me. Paris (show the flag), Marseille (show the ship), Lyon (silk), Bordeaux (grapes), Nice (flowers), and Lille (wool and coal).

"It's too bad, we don't seem to have anything in the middle. Well! Tomorrow, I'll tell you a wonderful, true story of a little boy and of his dog and we'll have a picture to pin in the middle.

"We'll stop our lesson now. Let's pretend I'm going to leave you (if you are the classroom teacher). . . . What do you think we will say to each other? Bonjour? No . . . We'll say . . . 'Au revoir.'

"You will say, 'Au revoir (Mademoiselle, Madame, Monsieur).' Again . . . 'Au revoir.'

"Bravo!"

A DREAM COME TRUE (UNIT 1) [2]

"Suddenly, one day, a dream the Girard family has had for a long time —of taking a trip to France—promises to come true. Let's go along with them, as they plan the trip and as they visit the storybook places in 'la belle France.' "

Picture 1:
Mr. Girard: Anne, Marie, Marc, venez ici.[3]

Picture 2:
Mrs. Girard: Me voilà, Robert. Qu'est-ce qu'il y a?

Picture 3:
Marie and Marc: Bonjour, papa. Qu'est-ce qu'il y a?

Picture 4:
Mr. Girard: Ecoutez. J'ai une surprise.
Family: Une surprise?

Picture 5:
Mr. Girard: Oui, une marveilleuse surprise. Nous allons en France.

Picture 6:
Family: En France! Oh, papa, quelle merveilleuse surprise!

Picture 7:
Mrs. Girard: Quand partons-nous?
Mr. Girard: Le quatre juillet.

Picture 8:
Mrs. Girard: Le quatre juillet? Ah, non! C'est impossible. Il y a trop de choses à préparer.

Picture 9:
Children: Oh, maman! Je t'en prie!

Picture 10:
Mr. Girard: Mais, voyons, Anne. C'est assez de temps. Regardons le calendrier.

[2] M. Pei and M. Finocchiaro, *French by Sight, Sound and Story* (recordings, illustrations, text), David McKay Company, Inc., New York, 1962.
[3] There are pauses for repetition after each word or logical segment.

Picture 11:
Mrs. Girard: Oui, regardons le calendrier. C'est aujourd'hui le vingt juin.
Picture 12:
Children: Et nous partons le quatre juillet. Nous avons encore quatorze jours. Ne t'inquiète pas, maman. Je vais t'aider!

MY FAMILY—OCCUPATIONS (TOPIC B) [4]

1. **Introduction** In preparation for this lesson the children are asked to bring in pictures illustrating men and women working at the various professions and occupations. If the children have been working with puppets, they can dress some of them to look like doctors, nurses, bakers, policemen, etc. In addition some members of the class may volunteer to make models of a grocery store, a butcher shop, a bakery, etc.

It is not necessary to teach all the vocabulary listed for this topic. Some of the occupations were listed for the benefit of the teacher, who may have to know the French equivalents when the children converse about what they will be when they grown up.

2. **Suggested Procedure**

a. The pictures representing the various occupations may be displayed as a frieze around the room. The models and puppets are easily accessible from a display table or a "boîte française."

b. In teaching the vocabulary, it is well to start with the words that sound similar in English such as "le docteur," "le dentiste," "le musicien," "le peintre," "le pilote d'avion," etc.

c. The simplest way to teach the new vocabulary is by pointing to the picture or model and by using the familiar pattern:

> Où est le dentiste?
> Voilà le dentiste.
> Où est le pilote d'avion?
> Voilà le pilote d'avion.

d. This can be varied with:

> Montrez-moi le tailleur.
> Voilà le tailleur.

---

[4] New York City Board of Education, *French for Elementary Schools*, Curriculum Guide, 1963. First year of instruction.

e. When the new vocabulary becomes familiar, the teacher may proceed with:

> Qui est le professeur?

and elicit

> Mlle Gordon est le professeur.
> Qui est médecin?
> Mon oncle est médecin.
> Qui est ingénieur?
> Mon père est ingénieur.

This will review the family vocabulary and reinforce the use of "mon," "ma," "votre," etc.

f. The children will enjoy answering the following question:

> Que serez-vous, quand vous serez grand(e)?

It is well for the teacher to give each child an opportunity to answer this question with:

> Quand je serai grand(e), je serai _____.

Special attention should be given to the pronunciation, since this sentence has many sounds that are peculiar to French.

g. The expression "chez" is very useful with this vocabulary.

> Où allez-vous?
> Je vais chez le médecin.
> Où allez-vous?
> Je vais chez le boulanger.

To dramatize this simple dialogue, use is made of the dressed puppets and models of the various stores. If this isn't practical, two or three children may sit up front and pretend to be "dentiste," "avocat," and "médecin" in individual offices. The teacher then walks toward each one saying:

> Je vais chez le médecin (le dentiste, l'avocat).

She then calls on children, who, in response to:

> Où allez-vous?

answer:

> Je vais chez le médecin (le dentiste, l'avocat).

3. Related Vocabulary and Patterns of Speech

le docteur	le boulanger	le fermier
le médecin	le tailleur	le pompier
le dentiste	l'épicier	l'agent de police
l'avocat	le boucher	le musicien
l'ingénieur	le facteur	le peintre
l'infirmière	le pilote d'avion	le commerçant
le pharmacien	l'hôtesse de l'air	le (la) dactyle
		le (la) secrétaire

Il est (médecin, ingénieur, pharmacien).
Où allez-vous?
Je vais chez _____.
Quand je serai grand(e), je serai.

4. Suggested Activities

a. One child is called on to name a profession or occupation. He then calls on another child to make up a French sentence using that word:

L'agent de police.
Mon oncle est agent de police.

b. Game. This is a form of charades. A child is called on to act out one of the occupations or professions. The rest of the class guesses who he is supposed to be.

PARLONS FRANÇAIS (LESSON 8) [5]

Before the Film Lesson In this lesson we learn to count up to fifteen. Then we see a scene in a French school: The teacher asks Gilbert where his book is and Gilbert doesn't know. Then the teacher, who has found the book, calls him forward and gives it to him. Gilbert returns to his seat a little noisily, and the teacher tells him to be quieter. The French school boys sing *Mon Merle*.

[5] *Parlons Français Teacher's Guide,* Heath deRochemont Corporation, Boston, Mass., 1962. Integrated materials: an example of television, films, recordings, and booklets for teachers and pupils.

Lesson Content
1. Numbers: onze, douze, treize, quatorze, quinze.
2. *Dialogue* (Teacher and Gilbert):
    T. Gilbert Laval, où est ton livre?
    G. Je ne sais pas, monsieur.
    T. Viens ici. Regarde!
    G. Ah, mon livre!
    T. Doucement, doucement!
3. Voilà un homme/un chien/une petite fille.
4. Song: *Mon Merle*

NEW MATERIAL
Numbers one–fifteen
ton livre/mon livre
Viens ici.
Doucement!
une petite fille

Student Record: Book 1, Record 4 (S4). Also Book 1, Record 5 (S5).
Activity Book: Lesson 8.

Classroom Procedure

1. Illustrate the difference between *ton* and *mon:* Holding a book with one hand point to it and to yourself with the other, saying, *Voilà mon livre.* Repeat. Then point to a book on the desk of a student, and then to him, saying, *Voilà ton livre,* repeating this procedure at least five times with other students. Come back to: *Voilà mon livre.* (Do not stress *mon* or *ton* in these sentences. French does not use the English stress pattern: "Here is *my* book.")

2. *Chain Practice:*

> Student 1: Jean (or other French name), où est ton livre? (Have students use each other's French names.)
> Student 2: Voilà mon livre.
> Student 1: Suzanne, où est ton livre?
> Student 2: Je ne sais pas.
> Student 1: Quel temps fait-il?
> Student 2: Il fait beau.

3. Drill numbers one–ten. Introduce eleven–fifteen in the same way as one–ten, repeating the numbers in sequence, then writing them out of sequence on the chalkboard.

4. Teach the dialogue between the teacher and Gilbert Laval. See page 16 [of the *Parlons Français Teacher's Guide*] for the recommended technique.

5. Sing *Mon Merle*.

Points

1. The *t* of *fait* is normally not pronounced. In *fait-il* it must be, and it is heard at the beginning of the second word: *"fai-til."* See Lesson 1, Point 1, for *liaison*.

2. *Doucement* is a useful classroom expression for telling students to slow down or quiet down. Its use need not be limited to the French lesson.

EXPRESSIONS DE TOUS LES JOURS [6]

DIALOGUE

—Qu'est-ce que c'est?
—C'est mon album de timbres-poste.
—Montre-le-moi. Ah, en voilà un joli!
—Oui, c'est un timbre français. J'en ai beaucoup.
—J'ai trois timbres espagnols. J'en échangerai un contre deux timbres français.
—Mais non. Ce n'est pas juste. Voici des timbres anglais. Tu en veux?
—Non, ils ne m'intéressent pas. J'en ai déjà. Regarde ces cartes postales. D'où viennent-elles?
—De la Russie. Ma tante m'en a envoyé.
—J'en voudrais une. Je vais écrire au Kremlin.

DIALOGUES ADAPTÉS

—As-tu vu le film sur la France hier?
—J'en ai vu un sur le palais de Versailles. Il est très intéressant, n'est-ce pas?
—Bien sûr. Je voudrais en voir un autre.
—Certainement, moi aussi.

—Nous avons une bonne équipe cette année.
—Je suis d'accord. Paul est un bon joueur.

[6] Marjorie Lowry Pei, *J'etudie le français* (Livret 2), McGraw-Hill Book Company, New York, 1963, pp. 31–32.

—Nous en avons trois—Paul, Henri, et Jean. Ce sont des champions.
—C'est la vérité.
—Tu as de nouveaux timbres-poste?
—Oui, j'en ai quatre.
—Moi, j'en veux un d'Espagne.
—Mon frère m'en a envoyé deux.
—Montre-les-moi. Ils m'intéressent beaucoup.
—Quel bruit! C'est une tasse qui est tombée?
—J'en ai cassé deux.
—C'est une catastrophe, Hier maman en a acheté quatre.
—Malheureusement, maintenant elle doit en acheter d'autres.

LET'S SPEAK SPANISH (UNIT 8) [7]

ASSOCIATION DRILL

Es mi casa.	It's my house.
Mi casa es bonita.	My house is pretty.
Mi casa es moderna.	My house is modern.
Mi casa no es vieja.	My house isn't old.

QUESTION–ANSWER DRILL

¿Qué es?	What is it?
Es una casa.	It's a house.
¿Dónde está tu casa?	Where is your house?
Mi casa está en _____.	My house is in _____.
¿Es bonita tu casa?	Is your house pretty?
Sí, mi casa es bonita.	Yes, my house is pretty.
¿Es moderna tu casa?	Is your house modern?
Sí, mi casa es moderna.	Yes, my house is modern.

STRUCTURE: SINGULAR OF "IR" VERBS: VIVIR

Pepe vive en (name of town).	Joe lives in _____.
El vive en _____.	He lives in _____.
María vive en una casa bonita.	Mary lives in a pretty house.
Ella vive en una casa bonita.	She lives in a pretty house.

[7] This unit is not complete. All elements in it are represented, however. From *Teacher's Guide, Let's Speak Spanish*, 1, by C. J. Schmitt. Copyright 1964. McGraw-Hill Book Company, New York. Used by permission.

RESPONSE DRILL

¿Dónde vive Pepe?	Where does Joe live?
¿Dónde vive él?	Where does he live?
¿Vive Paco en una casa moderna o vieja?	Does Frank live in a modern or an old home?
¿Vive María en España?	Does Mary live in Spain?

DIALOG

Niña 1: Hola, María. ¿A dónde vas?	Hello, Mary. Where are you going?
Niña 2: Voy a casa.	I'm going home.
Niña 1: ¿Dónde está tu casa?	Where is your house?
Niña 2: Aquí está mi casa.	Here's my house.

AUDIO–LINGUAL–VISUAL DRILL

1. ¿Qué es? — What is it?
   Es una casa. — It's a house.
2. ¿Es una casa vieja? — Is it an old house?
   Sí, es una casa vieja. — Yes, it's an old house.
3. ¿Es una casa moderna o vieja? — Is it a modern or an old house?
   Es una casa moderna. — It's a modern house.

After students have answered the questions above, have them talk about their own houses. Below is a guide as to what they might be expected to say.[8]

Mi casa está en (town). Es blanca y roja. Es bonita. No es vieja, es moderna. Es grande. Mi casa tiene seis cuartos: una sala, un comedor, una cocina, tres alcobas y un cuarto de baño.

¿QUE TAL? (UNIT 1) [9]

Filmstrip 1 On the first day of the school term, John and his sister Mary, walking along the sidewalk near the school, meet their friend

---

[8] Note from *Teacher's Guide.*
[9] Edin Brenes, Margaret Adey, George E. Smith, and James E. McKinney, *Learning Spanish the Modern Way,* Book 1, McGraw-Hill Book Company, New York, 1963, pages 25–28.

Sample Materials

George. With him is a boy whom they do not know. George introduces his friend Michael, who shakes hands with John and Mary. All three express pleasure at the meeting. Michael, in answer to John's question, says that he comes from Mexico.

DIALOG

Juan: Mira, María. Allí está Jorge. ¡Hola, Jorge!
María: ¿Qué tal?
Jorge: Buenos días. ¿Cómo están?
María: Estamos bien, gracias. ¿Y tú?
Jorge: Estoy bien, gracias.

REPETITION DRILL

Say the following sentences and repeat them:

1. ¿Dónde está Jorge?
2. ¿Dónde está él?
3. ¿Dónde está María?
4. ¿Dónde está su amigo?
5. ¿Dónde está su amiga?

PERSON SUBSTITUTION DRILL

Note that the following questions contain the words *¿dónde está?* and that all are alike except for the words at the end. Study the model, ask the questions, give the answers, and repeat them.

MODEL

Teacher: ¿Jorge?
Student: ¿Dónde está Jorge?
Teacher: ¿Dónde está Jorge?
Student: ¿Dónde está Jorge?

¿Dónde está | Jorge?
 | él?
 | María?
 | su amigo?
 | su amiga?

REPETITION DRILL

Give the following answers to the questions you have just learned and repeat them.

Allí está	Jorge.
	él.
	María.
	su amigo.
	su amiga.

QUESTION–ANSWER DRILL

Note that all the preceding answers contained *allí está* and were alike except for words at the end. Now, ask each question and give the entire answer, beginning with *allí está*.

MODELO (Model)
Teacher: ¿Dónde está Jorge?
Student: Allí está Jorge.
Teacher: Allí está Jorge.
Student: Allí está Jorge.

1. ¿Dónde está Jorge?
   Allí está Jorge.

2. ¿Dónde está él?
   Allí está él.

3. ¿Dónde está María?
   Allí está María.

4. ¿Dónde está tu amigo?
   Allí está mi amigo.

5. ¿Dónde está tu amiga?
   Allí está mi amiga.

REPETITION DRILL

In the answers note now a change to *está con*. Give first the question and then the answer and repeat both.

1. ¿Dónde está tu amigo?
   Mi amigo está con Jorge.

2. ¿Dónde está tu amigo?
   Mi amigo está con él.
3. ¿Dónde está tu amigo?
   Mi amigo está con María.
4. ¿Dónde está tu amigo?
   Mi amigo está con ella.

DIALOG

Juan: Jorge, ¿quién es tu amigo?
María: ¿Cómo se llama?
Jorge: Perdón. Quiero presentarles a mi amigo Miguel.
Juan: Mucho gusto, Miguel.
María: Mucho gusto, Miguel.
Miguel: El gusto es mío.
Juan: ¿De dónde eres?
Miguel: Soy de México.

REPETITION DRILL

Ask the following questions and repeat them:

¿Cómo se llama | tu amigo?
               | él?
               | tu amiga?
               | ella?

PERSON SUBSTITUTION DRILL

Note that the following questions contain the words *¿cómo se llama?* and that all are alike except for the words at the end. Ask the questions, substituting the new words, and repeat each sentence.

MODEL

Teacher: ¿Tu amigo?
Student: Cómo se llama tu amigo?
Teacher: ¿Cómo se llama tu amigo?
Student: Cómo se llama tu amigo?

¿Cómo se llama | tu amigo?
               | él?
               | tu amiga?
               | ella?

REPETITION DRILL

Say the following questions and answers and repeat both:

1. ¿Cómo se llama tu amigo?
   Mi amigo se llama Miguel.
2. ¿Cómo se llama él?
   El se llama Miguel.
3. ¿Cómo se llama tu amiga?
   Mi amiga se llama María.
4. ¿Cómo se llama ella?
   Ella se llama María.
5. ¿Cómo te llamas tú?
   Me llamo Miguel.
6. ¿Cómo te llamas tú?
   Me llamo María.
7. ¿Cómo se llama Ud.?
   Me llamo Miguel.
8. ¿Cómo se llama Ud.?
   Me llamo María.

The Verb Ser

REPETITION DRILL

Ask the following questions and repeat them:

¿De dónde es	su amigo?
	él?
	su amiga?
	ella?
	Jorge?

PERSON SUBSTITUTION DRILL

The following questions contain the words ¿de dónde es? They are all alike except for words at the end. Ask the questions, substituting the key words, and repeat each sentence.

MODELO

Teacher: ¿Su amigo?
Student: ¿De dónde es su amigo?
Teacher: ¿De dónde es su amigo?
Student: ¿De dónde es su amigo?

¿De dónde es | su amigo?
él?
su amiga?
ella?
Jorge?

REPETITION DRILL

Say the following questions and answers and repeat them:

1. ¿De dónde es su amigo?
   Mi amigo es de México.
2. ¿De dónde es él?
   El es de México.
3. ¿De dónde es su amiga?
   Mi amiga es de España.
4. ¿De dónde es ella?
   Ella es de España.
5. ¿De dónde es Jorge?
   Jorge es de los Estados Unidos.
6. ¿De dónde es Ud.?
   Soy de los Estados Unidos.
7. ¿De dónde es Ud.?
   Soy de Nueva York.
8. ¿De dónde eres tú?
   Soy de los Estados Unidos.
9. ¿De dónde eres?
   Soy de Nueva York.

Ejercicios Para Escribir In order to write correctly in Spanish, you must form some new habits. The written exercises in this book will help you form these habits, for in doing the exercises you will use the words and phrases that you already know.

Copy the dialog on page 173 three times. Notice the new habits that you must form in order to write in Spanish.

The conversation that you have copied is now given without punctuation or accent marks. Copy the dialog and supply what is missing.

Juan: Mira Maria Alli esta Jorge Hola Jorge
María: Que tal
Jorge: Buenos dias Como estan
María: Estamos bien gracias Y tu
Jorge: Estoy bien gracias

Complete las oraciones con la forma apropiada del verbo *estar*.

1. Allí está Jorge.
   ¿Dónde ___?___ María?
   ¿Dónde ___?___ su amigo?
   María ___?___ con Jorge.

2. Allí está él.
   ¿Dónde ___?___ Ud.?
   Yo ___?___ aquí.
   Juan y María ___?___ con Jorge.

3. Están con mi amigo.
   ¿Dónde ___?___ Uds.?
   Nosotros ___?___ con tu amigo.
   ¿Y tú, dónde ___?___?

4. María está bien.
   ¿Cómo ___?___ Jorge?
   ¿Cómo ___?___ Uds.?
   Nosotros ___?___ bien gracias. ¿Y tú?
   Yo ___?___ bien gracias. ¿Y él?
   El ___?___ bien. ¿Y María y Juan?
   Ellos ___?___ bien.

Copy the dialog on page 175 three times.

The conversation that you have copied is now given without punctuation or accent marks. Supply what is missing. Repeat this exercise until you can do it perfectly.

Juan: Jorge quien es tu amigo
María: Como se llama
Jorge: Perdon Quiero presentarles a mi amigo Miguel
Juan: Mucho gusto Miguel
María: Mucho gusto Miguel
Miguel: El gusto es mio
Juan: De donde eres
Miguel: Soy de Mexico

Cambie las siguientes oraciones según el modelo:

MODELO
¿Cómo se llama él? (Miguel)
El se llama Miguel.

1. ¿Cómo se llama ella? (María)
2. ¿Cómo se llama su amigo? (Jorge)
3. ¿Cómo se llama Ud.?
4. ¿Cómo te llamas tú?
5. ¿Cómo se llama él? (Juan)

Complete las oraciones con la forma apropriada del verbo *ser*.

El es de México.
¿De dónde __?__ él?
Ella __?__ de los Estados Unidos.
¿De dónde __?__ tu amigo?
Mi amigo __?__ de México.
¿De dónde __?__ tú?
Yo __?__ de Indiana.
¿De dónde __?__ Ud.?
Yo __?__ de los Estados Unidos.

POR LA MAÑANA (UNIT 4) [10]

Situation At 7:15 the children begin to get ready for school. After Paco and Enrique have washed themselves, Enrique thinks that Paco has put on his new shirt, but Paco tells him that it is on the bed.

[10] Modern Language Association, *Beginning Spanish, Grade 3, Teacher's Guide,* Educational Publishing Corporation, Darien, Conn., 1958.

Mamá has already ironed María's uniform and has put it in her room. María complains that Enrique has hidden her shoes. Mamá tells him to stop fooling and says it's time for breakfast.

Introduction

Cardboard clock
Cardboard bathroom, two bedrooms, kitchen
Paper-doll figures representing Mamá, Paco, Enrique, María
Clothes for these dolls: shirt, pajamas, girl's school uniform, shoes
Picture of children eating breakfast

IDENTIFICATION EXERCISE

Son las siete y cuarto.
Paco está en el baño.
Esta es una camisa.
Esta es una cama.
Estos son los dientes.
Este es el uniforme de María.
Estos son zapatos.
Estos niños están desayunando.

1. Basic Dialogue

A. Mamá   1   Levántate, Paco. Son las siete y cuarto.
   Paco   2   Ya me levanté. Estoy en el baño.
   Enrique 3   Termina pronto, chico. Tengo que lavarme.
   Paco   4   Ya estoy. Anda, lávate.
   Enrique 5   Paco, ¿por qué te pusiste mi camisa nueva?
   Paco   6   Esta no es tuya. Es mía. Mamá dejó la tuya sobre la cama.

   Mamá   1   ¿Te limpiaste los dientes, María?
   María 2   Todavía no, mamá, ya voy.
   Mamá   3   Ya te planché el uniforme. Lo tienes en tu cuarto.
   María 4   Mamá, Enrique me escondió los zapatos.
   Mamá   5   Enrique, déjate de bromas y bajen a desayunar.

B. ¿Qué hora es? Es la una y cinco. Son las dos y veinte.

2. **Suggested Procedures and Drills**   After the teacher has placed dolls representing Mamá in the kitchen, Paco in the bathroom, and Enrique at the bathroom door, she recites each line, using the dolls to indicate a change of speaker and the movement from one room to another.

Sample Materials

In the second part of the dialogue Mamá is in the kitchen and María speaks to her from the bedroom.

Individual children may now be called on to move the dolls while the teacher recites the lines. Other groups of children are called on to do the same, so that the class will have the experience of hearing the dialogue a number of times before repeating it. Then individual children may be prompted to repeat the lines.

When the situation is thoroughly familiar to them, sections of the classroom may be designated as the rooms of the house and the children are then prepared to dramatize the dialogue without using the dolls.

Continue this procedure until the lines are memorized.

3. Dialogue Adaptation

¿A qué hora te levantaste hoy?	Hoy me levanté a las siete.
¿A qué hora te levantaste ayer?	A las siete y media.
¿Dónde está Paco?	Está en el baño.
¿Dónde está la camisa de Enrique?	Está sobre la cama.
¿Dónde está el uniforme de María?	Está en el cuarto.
¿Qué están haciendo los ninos?	Están desayunando.
¿Qué es esto?	Una camisa.
¿Es tuya?	Sí, es mía.
¿Cuántas veces al día te limpias los dientes?	Dos veces.

4. Cumulative Exercise

RESPONSE DRILL

1. Paco ¿a qué hora te levantaste esta mañana? A las siete y media.
   ¿Te limpiaste los dientes? Sí, me los limpié.

2. ¿Qué tiempo hace hoy? Hace buen tiempo.
   ¿Hace frío o hace fresco? Hace fresco.
   ¿Te pusiste suéter o abrigo? Suéter.

3. ¿Qué es esto? Un rábano.
   ¿De qué color son los rábanos? Son rojos.
   ¿Te gustan? No mucho.

4. ¿Qué día es hoy? Es lunes.
   ¿En qué mes estamos? Estamos en octubre.

DIRECTED DIALOGUE

In this part and subsequent Directed Dialogues the teacher plays the part of the stage prompter. He selects two pupils, calls one by name and tells him what to say to the other pupil. If the pupil is unable to follow the directions, he gives him the actual words in a stage whisper. He continues this way through the dialogue. As the drill is repeated the prompting can be eliminated.

TEACHER	PUPIL
1. Pepe, pregúntale a Paco a qué hora se levantó esta mañana.	Pepe: Paco, ¿a qué hora te levantaste esta mañana?
Paco, contéstale que a las siete y media.	Paco: A las siete y media.
Pepe, pregúntale si se limpió los dientes.	Pepe: ¿Te limpiaste los dientes?
Paco, contéstale que sí, que te los limpiaste.	Paco: Sí, me los limpié.
2. Elena, pregúntale a Luisa qué tiempo hace hoy.	Elena: ¿Qué tiempo hace hoy, Luisa?
Luisa, contéstale que hace mal tiempo.	Luisa: Hace mal tiempo hoy.
Elena, pregúntale si hace frío o hace fresco.	Elena: ¿Hace frío o hace fresco?
Luisa, contéstale que hace frío.	Luisa: Hace frío.
Elena, pregúntale si se puso suéter o abrigo?	Elena: Luisa, ¿te pusiste suéter o abrigo?
Luisa, contéstale que abrigo.	Luisa: Abrigo.
3. María, esconde los lápices de Paco.	Pepe: Paco, ¿qué hizo María?
Pepe, pregúntale a Paco qué hizo María.	
Paco, contéstale que te escondió los lápices.	Paco: Me escondió los lápices.
Pepe, dile a María que se deje de bromas.	Pepe: María, déjate de bromas.

Sample Materials

MI CUADERNO DE ESPAÑOL (LESSON 3, THIRD DAY) [11]

Note. The numbers are an excellent means of teaching the new sounds. The first ten numbers contain all the vowels, four important diphthongs, and three of the four important consonants. See pages 254–257 of *Teaching Spanish in the Grades* for further help with these.

Purpose To pick up number leads in the story, and to show how Spanish numbers can be used in the classroom.

Props. Flannel board and cut-outs.

Use the greeting appropriate to the time of day, "Buenos días, niños," before noon; "Buenas tardes, niños," in the afternoon, to begin the Spanish class, but do not expect a reply yet.

Then, using "¿Cuántos?" and "¿Cuántas?" and explaining that it means "How many," lead back to the story by reviewing the names of all the things in the story, putting them back on the board as you do.

¿Cuántas sillas hay en la casa de los tres osos?
¿Cuántas camas hay en la casa de los tres osos?
¿Cuántas cucharas hay en la casa de los tres osos?
¿Cuántos platos hay en la casa de los tres osos?

Prompt the children with the correct answer, "Hay tres sillas, señorita," etc. Give them a feeling of success from the first. Let them know what you want. Strive for complete-sentence answers. Don't explain "hay" unless you are questioned about it. Accustom children to pronouncing and using it through oral mimicry and repetition. In order to avoid the English "hay" the written equivalent should not be shown to the children until pronunciation and habit of use are firmly fixed.

End this review with "¿Cuántas niñas hay?" The class replies, "Hay una niña." Point to the nearest niña and say, "Aquí hay una niña también. ¿Cuántas niñas hay en está fila?" Answer yourself by pointing to and counting the number of girls in the row you have chosen. Continue finding "las niñas" in the class and then transfer to "el niño." Continue pointing out and counting "los niños" until the need for knowing more than "uno," "dos," "tres" has been established.

Now count ten children yourself, beginning with a boy, and have them come to the front of the room, facing the class; the boy who is

[11] Margit W. MacRae, *Mi Cuaderno de Español,* Houghton Mifflin Company, Boston, 1959. Each lesson is carefully outlined. The "story" approach is featured.

"número uno" should be at the left of the class. "Uno" must become "una," if applied to a "niña," so be sure it is a "niño" who is "número uno." Refer to page 163 of Appendix 3 for Contando [of *Teaching Spanish in the Grades*], and play it for what remains of this lesson, ending it with the teacher saying, "Siéntese, por favor, número ocho," and so on, until all the ten are back in their seats.

End Spanish lesson with "Hasta mañana, niños," helping them say, "Hasta mañana, señorita."

Note. It is not too soon to begin using the everyday expressions in an actual situation. Try using "Hasta mañana" at dismissal as well as the sign-off of the regular Spanish lesson. The sooner the pupils find that Spanish is another means of talking to one another, the more fun it will be, and the more they will learn and remember.

CHILDREN'S LIVING SPANISH (LESSON 5) [12]

Record 1 . . . Side 1 . . . Band 5

Are your eyes bigger than your stomach? Helen's are! You'll never guess what she doesn't want. Mmmm.

Mamá: Vamos a comer ahora, Elena.
Elena: Si, mamacita, por favor. Ahora tengo mucha hambre. Son las diez y media ya.
Mamá: Yo lo sé. Levántate más temprano.
Elena: ¿Qué hay para mi desayuno?
Mamá: Una sorpresa.
Elena: ¿Una sorpresa? ¿Qué es? ¡Mmmmm! Panqués. ¡Qué bueno! Muchas gracias, mamacita.
Mamá: Siéntate a la mesa y ponte tu delantal.
Elena: ¿Dónde est mi delantal?
Mamá: Aquí está.
Mamá: ¿Qué quieres con los panqués, jarabe o mermelada?
Elena: Jarabe y mantequilla, mamá. Yo tengo mucha, mucha hambre.
Mamá: Hay tres más en este plato.
Elena: Los panqués son muy ricos, mamá, con jarabe y mantequilla.

[12] Mary Finocchiaro, *Children's Living Spanish*, Crown Publishers, Inc., New York, 1960. Records with pauses, accompanying books for children, teacher's manual, picture dictionary.

Mamá: ¿Qué quieres tomar —leche o chocolate?
Elena: Mm. Vamos a ver. Chocolate, por favor.
Mamá: Aquí está el chocolate y aqui hay tres panqués más.
Elena: Mamá, cómetelos tú. Son muy ricos.
Mamá: ¡Ja, ja! Elena, comes más con los ojos que con la boca.

    Vamos a cantar [13]
        Mamá is mother
        Ocho—eight
        Papá is father
        Tarde—late

SPANISH FOR CHILDREN (UNIT 11) [14]

Hoy es viernes.
Está sonando el teléfono.
El papá de Ana contesta.
Es para Ana.

Papá: Es para ti, Ana.
Ana: Es Pepe.
      Hola, Pepe.
      ¿Cómo estás hoy?
Pepe: Me siento mejor.
      Ya no tengo fiebre.
Ana: ¡Qué bueno!
Pepe: Vamos a ir al cine mañana.
      ¿Quieres ir?
Ana: Si, claro.
     ¿Qué dan?
Pepe: No sé. Es una película de vaqueros.
Ana: ¡Fantástico!
Pepe: Hasta mañana.

[13] Sung to the Spanish tune "Arroz con Leche." As children progress in their knowledge of the language, they enjoy composing the rhymes.
[14] F. Eddy (ed.), *Spanish for Children*, HRS Junior Language Hi-Fi Course (recordings), Ottenheimer Publishers, Baltimore, Md., 1957. Pauses are provided for repetition. Notice the *brief* conversational exchanges.

GROWING IN SPANISH (PROGRAM 9) [15]

"Buenas Tardes, amigos."
(Near map.) "¿Cómo están ustedes?" (Pause.)
"Muy bien, gracias."

Are you looking forward to your first school holiday? I guess we all are. It's nice to wake up on a Monday morning and to realize that we can stretch, and be lazy a little while longer.

But I wonder how many of us realize fully why October 12 is a holiday, not only in the United States but also in all countries throughout the Western Hemisphere where Spanish is spoken. Spanish-American people in North and South America have such a feeling of pride about the day that they have named it "El Día de la Raza"—The Day of the Race—meaning the Spanish-American Race, of course.

And they can well be proud, because it was thanks to the faith of the Spanish King and Queen, and more particularly of Queen Isabella, that a man's dream came true and that America was first settled by Europeans. It's difficult for us to grasp the fact that 500 years ago people on this side of the Atlantic didn't even know that this great country of ours existed. Even the Ocean was shrouded in mystery and was called by many "The Sea of Darkness." Some people weren't even convinced that the earth was round. They were sure that any ship sailing westward from Europe would sooner or later drop down into an unknown abyss.

There was one man, however, who didn't share the common beliefs. Cristóbal Colón, an Italian sailor living in Spain, whom we know as Christopher Columbus, after long years of study believed not only that the earth was round, but that by sailing west from Spain he could reach India, a land famous for its spices and treasures.

But he couldn't get anyone to believe in his idea. The King of Portugal had turned down his pleas for ships and men; the wise men

---

[15] This was a television program given on October 9, 1959, over WNYC in New York. The program, which may be used as a culminating activity, was prepared by the author with the cooperation of her husband, Dr. Santo Finocchiaro. You may wish to adapt this for an assembly program, using maps and simple props to which the narrator will point as he mentions the places or items.

The melody of the song was the familiar "Blow the Man Down."

Of course, more or less Spanish can be used, depending on all the variables we have discussed.

Sample Materials

of Spain had told the monarchs not to listen to Columbus's mad schemes. They were sure he was mad. Columbus had even appealed to the King of France. After years of knocking at many doors, Columbus was finally granted an audience with King Fernando and Queen Isabella.

The year is 1492. The scene—the beautiful Spanish palace in Granada.

And now I'd like you to close your eyes very tight for a moment. Try to let your imagination go back to the now well-known scene where Columbus asked Queen Isabella for sailors and ships to find the western route to India. Queen Isabella, as you know, was so touched by Columbus's plea that she gave him her personal jewels to help him fulfill his dream.

Open your eyes now and follow me with your eyes; not only with your eyes but also with your ears. I'm sure that you'll understand nearly all the Spanish you're going to hear.

"Bienvenido, Señor Colón. Venga usted. Diga lo que desea."

"Mi Reina, estoy aquí para rogarle a su Majestad me permita buscar una nueva y más directa ruta para las Indias. Estoy convencido de que la Tierra es redonda y que puedo llegar a las Indias navegando hacia el Oeste."

"¿Qué necesita usted, Colón, para este viaje?"

"Por lo menos tres carabelas y cien marineros."

"Bien, Colón, su plan parece bueno. Usted me ha convencido. Aqui están mis perlas. Puede pagar parte del viaje con estas perlas. ¡Valor y esperanza, Señor Colón, y buena suerte!"

"Le doy mil gracias, mi Reina y Señora. Con la ayuda de Dios, voy a darle un nuevo mundo para su gloria y la gloria de España."

"Bien Colón, adios—Vaya con Dios."

And so, Colón was promised sailors, money, and three caravels, or boats. But his troubles had just begun. The king had ordered that the city of Palos, as a punishment for some smuggling activities, should furnish two of the ships and the men. The people of Palos, frightened by the stories of sea dragons and black water, refused to prepare the ships or to sail. Finally, after many threats of imprisonment by the king, three ships were made ready: the Pinta, the Santa Maria, and the Niña. Men were pressed into service but they had purposely fixed the ships so that they would not hold up after a few days and Colón would be forced to turn back. And so it happened—Colón had to stay at the

Canary Isles for nearly six weeks while the Niña and the Pinta were being repaired.

Finally on September 9, the three caravels with Colón on the Santa Maria set sail for the unknown.

For days and days the frightened sailors saw nothing but empty sky and empty sea. They begged Columbus to turn back. When he refused and urged them to go on, they decided to mutiny and to throw him into the sea. For hours on end, the sailors' chant could be heard on the three ships: "We are tired of the endless voyage, of the cruelty of the sea. We are tired.—We must kill Cristóbal Colón." In Spanish it sounded like this (sung to the tune of "Blow the Man Down") :

"Cansados estamos, cansados de un viaje tan largo, sin fin.

"Ay, Ay, que crueldad!

"Estamos cansados de este viaje. Tenemos que matar a Colón."

Columbus knew how the sailors felt. He, too, was becoming disheartened at the fact that his calculations had not proved correct. He had been so sure that India was about 3000 miles away and that he should have sighted land long before this.

Finally, on the thirtieth day, he told the sailors that if at the end of three days they did not reach land, he would turn back.

That night Columbus was crouched over his maps, going over for the thousandth time the figures in the log that he had been keeping. He had been in despair with the sailors' chanting ringing in his ears. He closed his eyes and once more asked God for guidance. "Dios, mi Señor, Guíame, dame un consejo. Tú siempre sabes cuanto difícil es convencer a mis marineros!"

It seemed to him that a beautiful voice—was it the memory of Queen Isabella's or was it the voice of an angel sent by God—repeated, "Valor y esperanza, Colón. Siga siempre adelante." "Go ever forward, Columbus."

Colón awoke the next day renewed in spirit and urged his men onward. The very next day, signs that land must be near were seen. Was it a light in the distance they had seen? Could that possibly mean land? What are these pieces of wood floating on the sea, which has suddenly become very blue and very calm?

The excitement of the men knew no bounds when, early on the third morning, the sailor on watch yelled, "Tierra! Tierra!"

Land, long awaited, had been discovered. Columbus and the sailors knelt and offered a prayer to God.

Later, dressed in full uniform, carrying the banners of Spain, Co-

Sample Materials

lumbus went on the land to be greeted by the friendly people whom he called Indians because he thought he had discovered the Indies.

In a dramatic scene, he planted the flag of Spain on the Island and named it San Salvador, as a thanks to God. Then he took formal possession of the Island in the name of his sovereigns. From this first landing grew this wonderful new world in which we live.

GERMAN FOR CHILDREN (UNIT 6) [16]

Mutti: Heinz, zieh deinen Pullover an!
Heinz: Warum denn, Mutti?
Mutti: Es ist kalt draussen.
Heinz: Muss ich wirklich?
Mutti: Ja.
Heinz: Welchen soll ich denn anziehn?
Mutti: Den roten.
Heinz: Wo ist er denn?
Mutti: Sieh in deinem Zimmer nach.
Heinz: Ach, da ist er ja.

Vati: Hast du deinen Pullover, Bärbel?
Bärbel: Nein, Vati. Wo ist er denn.
Vati: Das weiss ich nicht. Sieh mal im Haus nach.
Bärbel: Vati, Heinz kann auf deutsch zählen.
Vati: Wirklich? Kann er noch was?
Bärbel: Ja natürlich!
Vati: Dein Bruder ruft!
Bärbel: Ich komme.

[16] F. Eddy (ed.), *German for Children*, HRS Junior Language Hi-Fi Course (recordings), Ottenheimer Publishers, Baltimore, Md., 1957. Pauses are provided for repetition. Notice the brief conversational exchanges. Note too that the second dialogue is an adaptation of the first one and a recapitulation of some language items which have been learned in previous units.

HEBREW FOR CHILDREN (UNIT 5) [17]

אִמָּא:	הָבָה נִסְפֹּר בְּעִבְרִית.		הַדּוֹד יוֹחָנָן: עַכְשָׁו סִפְרִי מִשֵּׁשׁ עַד עֶשֶׂר.	
שׁוֹשַׁנָּה:	שָׁלוֹם, הַדּוֹד יוֹחָנָן.		שׁוֹשַׁנָּה:	שֵׁשׁ 6
הַדּוֹד יוֹחָנָן:	שָׁלוֹם, שׁוֹשַׁנָּה.			שֶׁבַע 7
	מַה שְּׁלוֹמֵךְ?			שְׁמוֹנֶה 8
שׁוֹשַׁנָּה:	טוֹב, תּוֹדָה.			תֵּשַׁע 9
הַדּוֹד יוֹחָנָן:	הַאִם אַתְּ יוֹדַעַת לִסְפֹּר?			עֶשֶׂר 10
שׁוֹשַׁנָּה:	כֵּן, כַּמּוּבָן, הַדּוֹד יוֹחָנָן.		הַדּוֹד יוֹחָנָן: לֹא רַע לְגַמְרֵי!	
הַדּוֹד יוֹחָנָן:	בֶּאֱמֶת? הָבָה נִשְׁמַע.		הַגִּידִי לִי בַּת־כַּמָּה אַתְּ?	
	סִפְרִי מֵאַחַת עַד חָמֵשׁ.		שׁוֹשַׁנָּה: אֲנִי בַּת־שְׁמוֹנֶה.	
שׁוֹשַׁנָּה:	אַחַת 1			
	שְׁתַּיִם 2			
	שָׁלֹשׁ 3			
	אַרְבַּע 4			
	חָמֵשׁ 5			

Mother: Let's count in Hebrew.
Susan: Hello, Uncle John.
Uncle John: Hello, Susan. How are you?
Susan: Fine, thanks.
Uncle John: Do you know how to count?
Susan: Yes, of course, Uncle John.
Uncle John: Really? Let's hear. Count from one to five.
Susan: One 1
      Two 2
      Three 3
      Four 4
      Five 5
Uncle John: Now count from six to ten.

[17] F. Eddy (ed.), *Hebrew for Children*, HRS Junior Language Hi-Fi Course (recordings), Ottenheimer Publishers, Baltimore, Md., 1959. English translation of the Hebrew seems necessary because of the characters of the letters.

Sample Materials

Susan: Six   6
Seven   7
Eight   8
Nine   9
Ten   10
Uncle John: Not bad at all! Tell me, how old are you?
Susan: I'm eight.

ITALIAN FOR CHILDREN (UNIT 9) [18]

Mamma: Ebbene, dottore, che ha?
Il dottore: Una leggera infezione. Gli dia queste pillole.
Mamma: Può andare a scuola domani?
Il dottore: Domani, no. Forse martedì o mercoledì.
Mamma: Tante grazie, dottore.
Il dottore: Prego. Arrivederla.
Mamma: Arrivederla, dottore. Grazie di nuovo.

Maria: Giochiamo, Vittorio. Tu fai il dottore.
Vittorio: Bene.
Maria: Buon giorno, dottore.
Vittorio: Buon giorno. Che hai, non ti senti bene?
Maria: Sono così calda.
Vittorio: Certo, hai la febbre. Stai a letto oggi. Fuori fa freddo.
Maria: Posso andare a scuola domani?
Vittorio: Forse.
Maria: Arrivederla, dottore, e tante grazie.
Vittorio: Prego. Arrivederci.

[18] F. Eddy (ed.), *Italian for Children,* HRS Junior Language Hi-Fi Course (recordings), Ottenheimer Publishers, Baltimore, Md., 1957. Pauses are provided for repetition. Notice the brief conversational exchanges. Note too the use of the formal and informal forms within the same dialogue.

Sources and Resources for Teachers

An attempt to name all the texts and materials in the field of foreign language or second-language teaching would be foolhardy and a wasteful duplication. Every issue of professional journals contains one or more articles or references to texts, research studies, or sources of help for teachers. Therefore this section is limited to a brief, selective listing of bibliographies and professional texts (many of which contain extensive bibliographies) for further reading. Teachers are urged to obtain the bibliographies and, in addition, to subscribe to several of the professional journals indicated.

Interested personnel may obtain invaluable professional help from sources such as the Modern Language Association of America and its important arm, the Center for Applied Linguistics, the U.S. Department of Health, Education, and Welfare, and the British Council. It is desirable to obtain up-to-date brochures or catalogs of materials from these agencies at least once a year.

Grade guides and syllabuses, texts for children, and instructional materials, such as films, records, songs, games, wall charts, etc., are listed in several of the government publications mentioned. Most of these publications can be obtained for a nominal cost.

Elementary school teachers should also make extensive use of the sources and materials they use in other curriculum areas. For example, helpful free or inexpensive materials are often supplied by food companies or museums. Many books and magazines list sources of such materials, e.g., *The Instructor*.

Materials listed for secondary schools should also be considered. They can be adapted for younger children or used in the upper levels of the elementary school. More important, they help to promote the continuum in language teaching which should be a fundamental goal of teachers and administrators engaged in language teaching.

BIBLIOGRAPHIES AND MATERIALS LISTS

Alden, Douglas W. (ed.), *Materials List for Use by Teachers of Modern Foreign Languages,* Modern Language Association of America, New York, 1959.

Bibliography, British Council, London, England, 1963.

Eaton, E., M. Hayes, L. Norton, *Source Materials for Secondary School Teachers of Foreign Languages,* U.S. Department of Health, Education, and Welfare, Washington, D.C., OE 27001B, 1962.[1]

Glaude, Paul M., *Selective Guide to the Acquisition of Audio-Lingual and Related Materials Useful in Teaching Modern Foreign Languages in the "New Key,"* Chilton Company, Philadelphia, 1961.

Johnston, Marjorie, and Ilo Remer, *References on Foreign Languages in the Elementary School,* U.S. Office of Education, Washington, D.C., 1959.

Johnston, Marjorie, and Catherine Seerley, *Foreign Language Laboratories in Schools and Colleges,* U.S. Office of Education Bulletin 1959, no. 3, U.S. Government Printing Office, Washington, D.C., 1958.

Keesee, Elizabeth, *References on Foreign Languages in the Elementary School,* U.S. Office of Education Circular 495, U.S. Government Printing Office, Washington, D.C., 1960.

Lado, Robert, *Annotated Bibliography for Teachers of English as a Second Language,* U.S. Government Printing Office, Washington, D.C., 1955.

Modern Language Association of America, *FLES Packet,* Modern Language Association, New York, 1960.

O'Hannessian, Serarpi, *Interim Bibliography on the Teaching of English to Speakers of Other Languages,* Center for Applied Linguistics, Washington, D.C., 1960.

[1] This excellent recently issued brochure, for example, includes the following subheadings: Audio-Visual Aids, Course Outlines and Guides, Cultural Aids from Travel and Information Services, Evaluation and Testing, Foreign Language Association Journals, Foreign Language Newspapers, Instructional Aids (Games, Realia, etc.), International Understanding, Language Laboratories, Linguistics, Organizations Offering Professional Services, Professional Films and Tapes, Programmed Texts and Teaching Machines, Research Reports, Textbooks, Songs and Dances, Study, Travel, and Exchange for Students and Teachers, Vocational Opportunities.

Ollman, Mary (ed.), *MLA Selective List of Materials for Use by Teachers of Modern Foreign Languages in Elementary and Secondary Schools*, George Banta Company, Inc., Menasha, Wisc., 1962.

Lawrence Wylie and others, *Six Cultures (French, German, Hispanic, Italian, Luso-Brazilian, Russian)*. Selected and Annotated Bibliographies. Modern Language Association, New York, November, 1961.

PROFESSIONAL JOURNALS

Foreign Language Association Publications

Canadian Modern Language Review, Toronto, Canada.
Classical World, Fordham University, New York.
The French Review, Columbia University, New York.
German Quarterly, Syracuse University, Syracuse, N.Y.
Hispania, De Pauw University, Greencastle, Ind.
Italica, Boston University, Boston, Mass.
Modern Language Journal, St. Louis, Mo.
PMLA, Curtis Reed Plaza, Menasha, Wisc.
The Slavic and East European Journal, Brandeis University, Waltham, Mass.

Of Interest to Language Teachers

English Language Teaching, The British Council, London, England.
Language Learning: A Journal of Applied Linguistics, Ann Arbor, Mich.
Linguistic Reporter, Center for Applied Linguistics, Washington, D.C.
Modern Language Abstracts, Orange State Teachers College, Fullerton, Calif.
Bulletin, National Education Association, Department of Foreign Language, Washington, D.C.
PMLA, Modern Language Association of America, New York.

Miscellaneous Publications

The Instructor,[2] F. A. Owen Publishing Company, Dansville, N.Y.
Northeast Conference Reports, University Microfilms, Ann Arbor, Mich. Reports of annual conferences.

SERVICE BUREAUS

American Association of Teachers of French, National Information Bureau, Brooklyn College, Brooklyn, N.Y.

American Association of Teachers of German, Service Bureau, Colgate University, Hamilton, N.Y.

American Association of Teachers of Italian, Roosevelt University, Chicago, Ill.

---

[2] *The Instructor* features a very fine section on FLES in each issue.

American Association of Teachers of Slavic and Eastern European Languages (High School Russian Project Committee), Park Road Extension, Middlebury, Conn.

Hebrew Culture Service Committee for American Schools and Colleges, New York.

Service Bureau for Modern Language Teachers, Kansas State Teachers College, Emporia, Kan.

TEXTS—A BRIEF LIST

Andersson, Theodore, *The Teaching of Foreign Language in the Elementary School,* D. C. Heath and Company, Boston, 1953.

Belasco, S. (ed.), *Anthology,* D. C. Heath and Company, Boston, 1963.

Brooks, Nelson, *Language and Language Learning: Theory and Practice,* Harcourt, Brace & World, New York, 1960.

Cadoux, Remunda, *French for Secondary Schools,* New York State Department of Education, Albany, N.Y., 1962.[3]

Capretz, Pierre, *Audio-Lingual Techniques for Teaching Foreign Languages,* U.S. Department of Health, Education, and Welfare, Washington, D.C., 1962.

Dunkel, Harold B., and Roger A. Pillet, *French in the Elementary School: Five Years' Experience,* The University of Chicago Press, Chicago, 1962.

Finocchiaro, Mary, *Teaching English as a Second Language,* Harper & Row Publishers, Inc., New York, 1958.

Foreign Languages in Elementary Schools: Some Questions and Answers, Modern Language Association, New York, 1950.

Foreign Language Discussion Pamphlets, Modern Language Association, New York, 1960.

Foreign Language Programs in Elementary Grades, National Education Association, Education Research Service Circular 6, Washington, D.C., 1955.

Holton, King, Mathieu, Pond, *Sound Language Teaching,* University Publishers, New York, 1961.

Huebener, Theodore, *How to Teach Foreign Languages Effectively,* New York University Press, New York, 1959.

Huebener, Theodore, *Audio-Visual Techniques in Teaching Foreign Languages,* New York University Press, New York, 1960.

Huebener, Theodore, *Why Johnny Should Learn Foreign Languages,* Chilton Company, New York, 1961.

Hughes, Marie, and George Sanchez, *Learning a New Language,* Association for Childhood Education International, Washington, D.C., 1958.

Iodice, Don, *Guidelines to Language Teaching in Classroom and Laboratory,* Electronic Teaching Laboratories, Washington, D.C., 1962.

---

[3] Also available in Spanish and German.

Johnston, Marjorie C., and Catharine C. Seerley, *Foreign Language Laboratories in Schools and Colleges,* U.S. Department of Health, Education, and Welfare, Bulletin no. 3, Washington, D.C., 1959.

Johnston, M., I. Remer, and F. Sievers, *Modern Foreign Languages: A Counselor's Guide,* U.S. Department of Health, Education, and Welfare Publication 27004, Washington, D.C., 1960.

Keesee, Elizabeth, *Modern Foreign Languages in the Elementary School,* U.S. Department of Health, Education, and Welfare Bulletin no. 29, Washington, D.C., 1960.

Lado, Robert, *Language Teaching: A Scientific Approach,* McGraw-Hill Book Company, New York, 1963.

Lado, Robert, *Language Testing,* Longmans, Green and Company, New York, 1962.

Lado, Robert, *Linguistics across Cultures,* The University of Michigan Press, Ann Arbor, Mich., 1957.

The Language Laboratory, Modern Language Association Bulletin 39, New York, 1956.

Marty, Fernand L., *Language Laboratory Learning,* Wellesley, Mass., 1960.

McRae, Margit W., *Teaching Spanish in the Grades,* Houghton Mifflin Company, Boston, 1960.

Méras, Edmond, *A Language Teacher's Guide,* Harper and Row, Publishers, Incorporated, New York, 1962.

Mildenberger, Kenneth, *Status of Foreign Language in American Elementary Schools,* U.S. Office of Education, Reports, 1954 and 1955.

Modern Foreign Languages in the Comprehensive Secondary School, National Association of Secondary-School Principals, Washington, D.C., 1959.

O'Connor, Patricia, *Modern Foreign Languages in the Secondary School: Pre-reading Instruction,* U.S. Office of Education, no. 583, 1959.

Parker, William R., *The National Interest and Foreign Languages: A Discussion Guide and Work Paper,* U.S. Government Printing Office, Washington, D.C., 1957.

Pei, Mario, and Frank Gaynor, *A Dictionary of Linguistics,* Philosophical Library, Inc., New York, 1954.

Purchase Guide for Programs in Science, Mathematics and Modern Foreign Languages, Ginn and Company, Boston, 1959.

Some Solutions to Problems Related to Teaching of Foreign Languages in Elementary Schools, New York City Metropolitan School Study Council, New York, 1956.

Stack, Edward M., *The Language Laboratory and Modern Language Teaching,* Oxford University Press, Fair Lawn, N.J., 1960.

"A Symposium on Foreign Languages in the Elementary School," *NEA Journal,* vol. 49, Feb., 1960.

Teacher Guides of the Modern Language Association, Educational Publishing Corporation, Darien, Conn., 1958.

UNESCO, *Second Language Teaching in Primary and Secondary Schools,* vol. 13, no. 3, 1961.

INTEGRATED MATERIALS (STUDENT MATERIAL, DISCS, TEACHER'S MANUALS, ETC.)

ALM Programs (Mary Thompson, dir.), Harcourt, Brace & World, Inc., New York, 1962. Although intended primarily for secondary school, these should be studied.

Parlons Français (Anne Slack and others), Heath De Rochemont Corporation, Boston, Mass., 1962.

FL Program Notes
Standards for Teacher-education Programs in Modern Foreign Languages [1]

Prepared by a conference convened by the Modern Language Association in December 1963, this statement is addressed to state departments responsible for the certification of teachers and to institutions that prepare elementary- and secondary-school teachers of modern foreign languages. Its purpose is to identify and clarify acceptable standards of preparation.

1. Only selected students should be admitted to a teacher-preparation program, and those selected should have qualities of intellect, character, and personality that will make them effective teachers.

2. The training of the future teacher [2] must make him a well-educated person with a sound knowledge of United States culture, the foreign culture and literature, and the differences between the two cultures. It must also enable him to:

---

[1] Prepared by The Modern Language Association of America, no. 51, February, 1964.

[2] These specifications apply to the specialist in modern foreign languages at all levels. In the elementary schools there is a clear need for specialists as well as for the classroom teachers who do the follow-up work on the specialist teacher's lesson.

       a. Understand the foreign language spoken at normal tempo.
       b. Speak the language intelligibly and with an adequate command of vocabulary and syntax.
       c. Read the language with immediate comprehension and without translation.
       d. Write the language with clarity and reasonable correctness.
       e. Understand the nature of language and of language learning.
       f. Understand the learner and the psychology of learning.
       g. Understand the evolving objectives of education in the United States and the place of foreign-language learning in this context.

    3. In addition to possessing the requisite knowledge and skills, the language teacher must be able to:
       a. Develop in his students a progressive control of the four skills (listening, speaking, reading, writing).
       b. Present the language as an essential element of the foreign culture and show how this culture differs from that of the United States.
       c. Present the foreign literature effectively as a vehicle for great ideas.
       d. Make judicious selection and use of methods, techniques, aids, and equipment for language teaching.
       e. Correlate his teaching with that of other subjects.
       f. Evaluate the progress and diagnose the deficiencies of student performance.

    4. An approvable program to prepare such a teacher must include:
       a. Intelligent evaluation and utilization of his pre-college language training through course placement according to results of proficiency tests.
       b. An offering of language and literature courses advanced enough to enable him to teach the gifted student.
       c. Courses and directed reading that give him a first-hand acquaintance with major works of literature, to be tested by a comprehensive examination.
       d. Use of the foreign language as the language of instruction in all language and literature courses.
       e. Extensive and regular exposure to several varieties of native speech, through teachers, lecturers, discs, tapes.

- *f.* Instruction in the foreign geography, history, and contemporary culture.
- *g.* Instruction in stylistics, phonetics, and linguistics.
- *h.* Instruction in the psychology of language learning.
- *i.* Instruction and practice in the use of the language laboratory and audio-visual aids.
- *j.* Systematic observation of the foreign language being expertly taught, followed by the experience of teaching under expert direction.
- *k.* Evaluation of the teacher candidate through (1) proficiency and other appropriate tests, (2) appraisal of his teaching skill by experts.

5. An approvable program should *also* make provision for:
   - *a.* Native speakers as teachers or informants.
   - *b.* Study abroad for at least one summer.
   - *c.* Organized extra-curricular foreign-language activities.
   - *d.* Development of interest in and ability to interpret research results.

Glossary of Useful Terms

Some of the following terms used in the text may also have other meanings. The definitions or explanations given here are limited to those needed in the context of a FLES program.

Action Series—also called the Gouin Series: a type of learning method in which children in groups or as individuals perform a series of sequential actions and say what they are doing as they perform each action.
active vocabulary: the content and function words of a language which are learned so thoroughly that they become a part of the child's understanding, speaking, and later, reading and writing vocabulary. [*See also* passive (recognitional) vocabulary.]
approach: (1) the introduction to a unit of work or to the intensive study of language items through procedures or devices that motivate children by establishing the need for learning, e.g., a song, dialogue, fairy tale, film, recording; (2) a synonym for "method," e.g., the audio-lingual approach or the aural-oral approach.
articulation: (1) the smooth continuous sequence from one learning level to another; (2) the meeting points of the vocal organs in the production of sounds.
audio-lingual: (1) listening and speaking; (2) the widely used name for the linguistic approach to teaching through listening, speaking, and intensive pattern practice. Other terms for audio-lingual are aural-oral and audio-oral.
backward build-up: a technique for teaching utterances of more than six or seven segments. Breaking them from the end into small logical segments helps teachers and children maintain the appropriate intonation. Each

segment is modeled by the teacher and repeated by the students. After the individual segments are learned, the entire utterance is repeated.

center of interest: a topic or theme on which teacher and children focus their attention for one or more lessons, e.g., greetings, shopping for food, a holiday. The center of interest serves as a setting for the presentation and intensive practice of language items and patterns while giving insight into social or cultural features of a language community.

chain drill: a type of pupil activity in the language classroom. After the teacher models a statement, one student repeats it, then the student seated next to him repeats it, then the student seated next to the second student repeats it, etc., until about eight children have participated. Chain drills can be used effectively in question and response drills, in substitution exercises, in adding to previous sentences, and in many other practice activities.

choral recitation: repetition of any language material by the entire class or by a group speaking together. Where feasible, choral recitation should always precede individual recitation.

communication: (1) the ability to understand, to speak to and respond to another individual. The response may be varied, e.g., answering a question, making a statement, performing an action, carrying out a request, or using a formula, such as "You're welcome." (*See also* interaction.)

content word: a word that is used to describe a thing, an action, or a quality, e.g., "pencil," "buy," "yellow." The vocabulary of a language is made up of thousands of content words. (*See also* function word.)

contrived material: reading material prepared by individuals or committees in which unfamiliar language items are interspersed among known words. Children are helped to guess at the meaning of the new words from the surrounding familiar words. Contrived material should be used as a third step in the development of reading skills. The first two types of materials used in reading should be (1) basic utterances, sentences, dialogues, songs, etc., which duplicate sentences, dialogues, and songs which have been learned thoroughly audio-lingually and (2) recombined utterances or sentences. (*See also* recombination dialogue or reading.)

correlation: (1) the act of bringing together learnings from one or more subject areas with the foreign language for their mutual enrichment; (2) the use of various language skills (listening, speaking, reading, or writing) in authentic communication situations.

cue: a word, picture, or gesture that stimulates the desired response.

culminating activity: a play, quiz show, festival, party, assembly program, interclass demonstration, preparation of an exhibit, etc., which marks the completion of a unit of work and which includes all or some of the material learned during the study of that unit.

culture: the values, beliefs, mores, traditions, art forms, and language of a community or a society.

cultural island: the total immersion of the foreign language class into the foreign culture through the continuous use of the language of that culture, the display of its authentic materials, the listening to its speakers, and any other activity that duplicates an activity in the foreign land.

cultural pluralism: (1) the social philosophy which emphasizes that the culture of countries such as Canada and the United States is the product of the cultures of the varied immigrant groups which people them; (2) the social philosophy which urges that immigrant groups retain their cultural heritage (in consonance with the limitations or features of the new environment) and thus contribute to the richness and variety of the country to which they have come.

diorama: a miniature stage setting in which lifelike scenes are created (farms, stores, streets, historical events) through paintings or the use of appropriate small objects.

equivalent: words or expressions in one language that convey the same meaning in another language although they are not word-by-word translations of each other, e.g., French: "Il y a une heure que je parle."/English: "I have been speaking for an hour."

experience chart: several utterances in the children's own words telling of a trip they have taken or of any other activity in which they have engaged. These sentences are written by the teacher on a piece of oaktag or on the blackboard and are used later as initial reading material.

FLES: widely used abbreviation for Foreign Languages in Elementary Schools.

follow-up activities: experiences such as drills, songs, and dramatization of dialogues in which children participate in order to practice language items that have been presented.

formula: expression normally used by native speakers of a language in social situations, e.g., "How do you do?" "I don't mind at all."

function word: a word which does not describe a thing, quality, or action, but which is used only to convey grammatical relationships, e.g., prepositions and auxiliary verbs.

informant: an individual who is a native speaker of a language or who has near native ability. The informant helps conduct drills and prepare instructional materials although he is not a trained teacher.

in-service program: a school or community teacher-training plan that may include such activities as seminars, workshops, bulletins, television, or films for individuals who are already teaching. The program is designed to increase their competency or to bring them abreast of new developments.

integration: the process of bringing together related materials, e.g., language items and cultural situations in which the items can be used logically.

interaction: (1) a synonym of "communication"; (2) the response to a previous speaker by words, gestures, or actions.

interchange: a brief dialogue of two or more utterances between two or more children.

intonation: the melody of a language produced by the rise and fall of the voice.

language arts also called language skills: a term that includes the abilities to understand, speak, read, and write a language.

language laboratory: a room or part of a room equipped with at least one tape recorder, microphones, and tapes where children listen to and imitate material on a tape. At later levels of language learning, the laboratory can be used effectively for pattern practice exercises.

level: a stage of language learning. For example, children starting a language are said to be at the beginning level. Many consider the foreign language program in the elementary school the beginning or elementary level. The work of FLES "graduates" at the secondary school may then be termed the intermediate or secondary level.

linguistic science: the body of knowledge that analyzes and describes the system of language. It is concerned with the sounds, grammar, and vocabulary of a language.

model: a basic utterance or pattern spoken by the teacher or a native speaker either live or on tape which children imitate.

native speaker: a person born in the language community or one who has learned the language (including its gestures) so thoroughly that he could be mistaken for a native.

pattern: a recurring arrangement of sounds, forms, words, utterances, or sentences in a language. Other sound, word, or form arrangements that fit into the slots of a known pattern permit speakers to create infinite numbers of additional utterances. (*See also* slot.)

passive (recognitional) vocabulary: the words of the language which the language learner understands (when heard or read) but which he has not learned to use in speaking or writing. (*See* active vocabulary.)

pattern practice: a drill or exercise designed to give learners intensive repetition of a language item. The practice may consist of repetition of a model, or it may involve substitutions, additions, deletions, or combinations of words in the model or pattern being learned.

pause: one feature of pronunciation of a language. It refers to the transition between sounds, e.g., night rate/nitrate, or to the fade-out of the voice at the end of an utterance.

prompt: to whisper to the learner a word, expression, or utterance that appears to be causing him difficulty. Prompting should be done quickly—in order to retain the brisk or smooth pace of a drill—and unobtrusively.

pronunciation: the sound system of a language, including vowel and consonant sounds, intonation, rhythm, stress (if any), and pause.

recombination dialogue or reading: a number of learned utterances used (1) with other varied, feasible, known words, (2) in a sequence that differs from the one in which they were originally learned, (3) with known utterances from other units, (4) in a cultural setting different from the one in which they were previously presented.

reentry: the deliberate use of language items that have been studied in new material or in another activity into which they fit logically in order (1) to keep them alive in the minds of the learners and (2) to give extensive practice in them in many communication situations.

reintroduction: a synonym for "reentry."

rejoinder: a reply to a question, statement, or action. The rejoinder may be another question, a statement, or an utterance of any kind.

rhythm: a feature of the sound system of the language. The characteristic rhythm of a language is produced by the regular repetition of its stressed syllables.

slot: the position of a word or phrase in an utterance that could be occupied by words or phrases of the same class; e.g., in "I'm going to the library," the slot "to the library" can be replaced by "to the store," "to the park," "to the hospital," etc.

spiral approach: a method of teaching in which the same language item or cultural topic is presented in greater depth at each succeeding level of learning.

stress: (1) a feature of pronunciation; (2) the prominence of syllables or words in the sound system of the language. In English, stressed syllables are usually longer and louder than other syllables.

structure: (1) a word sometimes used as a synonym for "grammar" or for "pattern"; (2) the system of sounds, words, forms, and word arrangements of a language.

symbol: a representation of something else. For example, the symbol [a] in the International phonetic alphabet represents the sound of ă in "hat"; the spelling b/r/e/a/d stands for the sounds b/r/ɛ/d; the word "bread" represents an item of food made with flour and water.

system: the recurring patterns of sounds, word forms, and word arrangements in a language that distinguish it from any other language.

target language: a foreign language that is being learned or taught.

track: a pattern of subject organization or of course sequences in a school. For example, at the beginning level in elementary school, there might be two tracks: one for very gifted children and the other for less able children. At the secondary level, there may be two or even three tracks in a foreign language: In one track may be children who have studied the language; in the second may be children who have not studied the language; in a third may be children who had not made satisfactory progress in the elementary school and who need a special curriculum.

transfer: the ability to use knowledge of some feature of one's native language or of the target language in learning another feature of the target language. Transfer of learning is not generally automatic. Teachers should point out transferrable features (sounds, forms, words) which would facilitate learning.

utterance: a word, expression, or sentence that conveys full meaning. An utterance does not have to be a complete sentence. For example, the utterance "John" would be a perfectly normal response to the question "Who ate lunch with you?" Formulas of the language, e.g., "certainly" and "of course," are utterances. It is important in teaching not to insist on complete sentences when the normal response in real communication would be a one-word utterance.

vocal: sounds made by the organs (lips, tongue) in the mouth.

Index

Action series, teaching of, 63
Activities in classroom, aural, 88
   oral, 89, 90
   reading and/or writing, 90–92
Anthropological sciences, principles derived from, 30
Approaches in skill development, 58–65
   (*See also* Language teaching)
Articulation with secondary schools, 14, 135–140
Audio-lingual skills, development of, 67–80, 88–92
   classroom activities fostering, 88–92
   pattern practice in, 72–80
   sequence in, 66, 67, 151, 152

Bibliographies, 193, 194
Blackboard, uses of, 130–132
British Council, 194

Centers of interest, 38–41
   (*See also* Cultural topics)
Child learning, advantages of, 4
College programs and teacher recruitment, 8, 9
Communication, definition of, 37
Community, language in, 7
   participation of, 18, 19
   utilizing resources in, 125–127
Costs of program, 18

Cultural island in the classroom, 94–96
Cultural topics, integration with language items, 56, 57
   list of, 38–41
   teaching of, 50–51
Culture, definition of, 24, 26
   foreign, developing appreciation of, 86–88
Curriculum, elementary school, 35, 36
   FLES (*see* FLES program)
Curriculum planning, informant's role in, 10
   teacher's role in, 21

Dialogues, as an approach to learning, 59–61
   illustrations of, 119, 120, 159–161
   sample, 159–161
   teaching of, 59–61
Dunkel, Harold, 67

Elementary school curriculum, developmental stages in, 35, 36
FLES in, 12, 36, 132–135, 146
Evaluation, 135–140, 147, 148
   use of tape recorder in, 123

Flannel board, uses of, 117–119
FLES program, characteristics of desirable, 20

FLES program, checklist for curriculum writers, 155–156
  curriculum, 38–46
  in elementary school curriculum, 12, 36, 132–135, 146
  and national needs, 6
  preparing a guide, 141–155
  special problems, choice of language, 17
    in Canada, 7
    in southwest United States, 7
    costs, 18
    credit, granting of, 14
    deferment of language study for non-English speakers, 7
    selection of pupils, 6, 7
    teacher shortage, 8–11
    time in the school day, 12, 14
    starting point, 12, 13
Format, Language Guide (*see* Language Guide)
Fries, Charles, 27

Games, 105–112
Glossary of terms, 201–206
Gouin, François, 63

Informants, role of, 10
International Phonetic Alphabet (IPA), 154

Journals, professional, 194

Kluckhohn, Clyde, 25

Laboratory, uses of, 122–124
Language, in community, 7
  and culture, 24
  definition of, 22
  as learned behavior, 23, 27, 143–146

Language, spoken, primacy of, 23
  system in, 27, 144
Language Guide, preparation of, 148–155
Language learning, activities producing, 88–93
  conflict with native language in, 21
  linguistic principles and, 26–28
  objectives of, 24–26
  psychological principles and, 24
  transfer in, 25
Language teaching, approaches in skill development, 58–65
  action series, 63
  dialogue, 59–61
  incidental happenings, 64–65
  reading material, 65
  situational learning, 63–64
  songs, 62, 63
  storytelling, 61–63
  cultural topics in, 50, 51, 56, 57
  developing appreciation of foreign culture, 86–88
  developing audio-lingual skills, 67–80, 88–92
    grading structures, 49, 50, 53–55
    pattern practice, 72–80, 82, 83
    pronunciation, 83–85
  developing reading skills, 80–82, 90–92
  developing writing skills, 82–84, 90–92
  English, use of, in, 28, 31
  patterns in, 27, 43–46
  psychological principles in, 29
  relationships, establishing pleasant class, 97–99
  selecting items for, 31
  spiral approach in, 28, 53–55
  of structures, 49–55, 63, 65, 85–87, 145–147
  variety of materials and techniques in, 105–135
  of vocabulary content, 46–49, 55
Linguistic science, principles derived from, 26–28, 143–146

McRae, Margit, 61, 150
Modern Language Association, "Standards for Teacher-Education Programs," 198–200
 starting point of materials prepared by, 13
Motivation, importance of, 29, 104
Movies, uses of, 124

Notebooks of children, 129, 130

Pattern practices, 72–80, 82, 83
 drills, directed practice, 78, 79
  expansion, 76, 77
  integration, 77, 78
  progressive replacement, 76
  question-and-answer, 73–74
  reduction, 77
  repetition, 73
  replacement, 74, 75
  substitution, 74
  transformation, 75–76
  translation, 79
 stimuli in, 72, 73
 techniques in conducting, 99
Pictures, list of, 113–116
 use of, 112–116
Pillet, Roger, 67
Planning for teaching, 100–105
 lesson planning, 103–105, 153, 154
 unit planning, 100–103
  dividing a unit of work, 101–103
Play activities, 119, 120
Pocket chart, preparation and uses of, 127, 128
Pronunciation, teaching of, 83–85, 143, 144
Props, uses and list of, 116, 117
Psychological sciences, principles derived from, 28–30
Pupils, exclusion of, 7
 reporting achievements of, 139, 140
 selection of, 6
Puppetry, 120, 121

Radio, uses of, 124
Reading, development of skills, 80–82
 initial, 80
 introduction of, 28, 66, 67
 procedures in teaching, 81, 82
 and teaching of structures (*see* Structures)
 testing comprehension in, 138
Recruitment of teachers, 8–11
Repetition, choral, techniques in, 69, 70
Reporting achievement of pupils, 139, 140

Secondary schools, articulation with, 135–140
 choice of language in, 14–16
 multiple tracks in, 14–16
Selection, of language, 17
 of pupils, 6
Service bureaus for teachers, 194, 195
Songs, teaching of, 62, 63, 121
Spiral approach in teaching, 28, 36, 47, 48, 53–55, 129, 130
Storytelling, 61–63
Structures, for emphasis, 41–46
 grading of, 49, 50
 integration with cultural topics, 56, 57
 teaching of, 49–55, 63, 65, 85–87, 145–147
Student-teachers, role of, 8, 9

Teacher-education programs, standards for, 198–200
Teacher-training, role of specialist in, 9
 television in, 9
Teachers, development of competency in, 11, 12, 32, 33
 qualifications of, 11
 recruitment of, 8–11
 role in beginning classes, 11, 30–33
 service bureaus for, 194, 195

Teachers, standards for, 198–200
Team-teaching, 8
Television, in teacher-training, 9
   in teaching children, 124
Testing, 135–140
   insuring success in, 136, 137
   of language skills, 135–140
     aural comprehension, 137
     oral production, 137, 138
     reading comprehension, 138, 139
     writing ability, 138
Time schedules, 12

Utterance, definition of, 27

Vocabulary, selection and teaching, 27, 46–49, 55, 144, 145
Vocabulary wheel, 128, 129

Writing, development of skill, 82–84
   introduction of, 28, 66, 67
   testing of, 138